Ashram Diary

In India with Bede Griffiths

First published by O Books, 2009
O Books is an imprint of John Hunt Publishing Ltd., The Bothy, Deershot Lodge, Park Lane, Ropley,
Hants, SO24 0BE, UK
office1@o-books.net
www.o-books.net

Distribution in:

UK and Europe
Orca Book Services
orders@orcabookservices.co.uk
Tel: 01202 665432 Fax: 01202 666219
Int. code (44)

USA and Canada
NBN
custserv@nbnbooks.com
Tel: 1 800 462 6420 Fax: 1 800 338 4550

Australia and New Zealand
Brumby Books
sales@brumbybooks.com.au
Tel: 61 3 9761 5535 Fax: 61 3 9761 7095

Far East (offices in Singapore, Thailand,
Hong Kong, Taiwan)
Pansing Distribution Pte Ltd
kemal@pansing.com
Tel: 65 6319 9939 Fax: 65 6462 5761

South Africa
Alternative Books
altbook@peterhyde.co.za
Tel: 021 555 4027 Fax: 021 447 1430

Text copyright Thomas Matus 2008

Design: Stuart Davies

ISBN: 978 1 84694 161 0

A CIP catalogue record for this book is available
from the British Library.

Printed by Digital Book Print

O Books operates a distinctive and ethical publishing philosophy in
all areas of its business, from its global network of authors to
production and worldwide distribution.
This book is produced on FSC certified stock, within ISO14001
standards. The printer plants sufficient trees each year through
the Woodland Trust to absorb the level of emitted carbon in
its production.

Ashram Diary

In India with
Bede Griffiths

Thomas Matus

BOOKS

Winchester, UK
Washington, USA

CONTENTS

Introduction

Meeting Bede Griffiths

This diary is about living with a guru in India. It is also about Christian spirituality, since the guru, Dom Bede Griffiths[1] (1906–1993) was a Christian, and his ashram is part of the Benedictine Order: a confederation of monasteries that follow the sixth-century Rule attributed to Benedict of Nursia. The ashram, founded in 1950 by two French priests, Jules Monchanin and Henri Le Saux, is in the southern Indian state of Tamil Nadu and is usually called Shantivanam, which means 'forest of peace.'

Dom Bede was, for me and for the whole world, an example of the incorporation of India's spiritual traditions into Christianity and of the Church into India. This is neither syncretism nor proselytism: it is integration at the deepest possible level, 'in the cave of the heart.'

My own time in the ashram has been intermittent; mostly, I have lived as a monk in Italy and the United States. While I was a novice monk, I read Bede Griffiths' autobiography, *The Golden String*: the story of his discovery of God in Nature and in Christ, and his monastic initiation at the abbey of Prinknash in England.

We met in Rome in 1979; he had come to propose affiliating the ashram with the Holy Hermitage of Camaldoli in the mountains of central Italy, a Benedictine community in whose historical origins Dom Bede found the closest Christian analog to India's ashrams. He and the young Indian brothers with him became members of our monastic congregation, the Camaldolese Benedictines.

Dom Bede had been in India since 1955. Together with a Belgian Trappist, he founded a monastery of the Syrian-Catholic rite in the mountains of Kerala to the west of Tamil Nadu. Dom

Bede went to Shantivanam in 1968, and although very little had been built there, he always referred to Monchanin and Le Saux as 'our founders' and venerated their memory.

Ashram is a Sanskrit term becoming common in English usage. It denotes either a stage in life (according to the classical Hindu conception of castes and initiations), or a place of abode — the hermitage of a spiritual master (guru) who may or may not have disciples with him.

Jules Monchanin, a priest of the diocese of Lyon in France, did not think of himself as a guru, but Shantivanam came into existence because of him. Born in 1895 and ordained in 1922, he dedicated his life to rethinking Christianity according to non-Western cultural paradigms. In 1939 he went to India with the express intention of living as a Christian hermit among the poor of Tamil Nadu. Dom Henri Le Saux, a Benedictine monk of the abbey of Kergonan in Brittany, wrote to Monchanin shortly after the Second World War. Le Saux joined him in 1948, and on the feast of Saint Benedict in 1950, in a mango grove by the sacred river Kaveri, they began a form of ascetical and contemplative life, unknown among Indian Christians.

India's traditions, both Hindu and Buddhist, give us many examples of monastic life. If you look for what is behind them, I believe you will find two ways of being a monk or a nun — two archetypes, you might call them. The first is the way of total renunciation (sannyasa in Sanskrit) and separation from all that is connected with ordinary human existence, including external religion and conventional ethics. The second is the way of yoga: transcendence through integration, which aims at pacifying all human impulses, including the impulse to renounce, and overcoming or unifying polarities and pairs of opposites.

To be a monk is to seek God, says Saint Benedict. To this basic criterion of his Rule, you can add another: the monastic life is also a search for new cultural horizons. It is a search for meaning beyond the boundaries — geographical and chronological — of my native culture, because no culture is sufficient unto itself. "No man is an island," said John Donne and Thomas Merton, and I am not the monk I am called to be if I do not plunge down my coastal shelf and through the depths, to reconnect with rising land that leads to another, farther shore.

A sannyasi is one who has cast aside the world, but he is also cast aside by the world. His clothing is ideally 'the yellow dust and the wind,' that is, he is naked. Custom has allotted him clothes the color of dust and fire, kavi, which may be anything from pale yellow to saffron to bright reddish-orange. He has no fixed abode; he begs his food. Monchanin and Le Saux came as close to this ideal as church laws of the time would allow, and above all they chose to live in the poverty and simplicity of the nearby villagers. They began the construction of a place of worship along the lines of a small, rural temple — the images of Hindu mythology being replaced by similar figures from the Christian apocalypse, the book of Revelation. They also adopted new names: Monchanin became Swami Parama-Arubi-Ananda ('he whose joy is in the supreme Spirit'), and Le Saux became Swami Abhishiktananda ('he whose joy is in the Anointed One, the Christ').

Monchanin and Le Saux also called their abode Saccidananda Ashram, or the Ashram of the Trinity. Saccidananda is a term from Vedanta philosophy and signifies the three qualities, being-consciousness-joy, of the transcendent Absolute, Brahman. Many Christian writers, including the founders of Shantivanam, have applied this term to the mystery of the Trinity. 'Being' is attributed to the Father — the unoriginated origin in God. 'Consciousness' is assigned to the Eternal Word — the Logos, and 'Joy' to the Holy Spirit.

Monchanin died in 1957, and Le Saux, Abhishiktananda, took to the road, spending months in the itinerant lifestyle of the sannyasis. But there was one Hindu monk (not a wanderer but a hermit), who inspired Abhishiktananda more than any other,

Ramana Maharshi, the greatest modern saint of Tamil Nadu and guru of an ashram at the foot of the sacred mountain Arunachala. Abhishiktananda met him twice before he died in 1950 and often returned to the mountain for long retreats. In 1968, Abhishiktananda chose to dwell permanently as a hermit in northern India, near the source of the Ganges, and Bede Griffiths came to take his place at Shantivanam. Swami Abhishiktananda died in 1973.

During the summer of 1984 I made my first retreat at Shantivanam. There I saw how Bede Griffiths incarnated the monastic ideal — the hermit, the sannyasi — and reinterpreted it, theoretically and practically. In him, renunciation and integration were one and the same thing, and he showed me how the ideal of another age can have life today and enliven those who are called to it. I also discovered — through their writings and the stories I heard from those who knew them — the other two hermits of Saccidananda, Monchanin and Le Saux. The latter, Abhishiktananda, was the first of the two I read; he seemed very real and near. But after Dom Bede's death in 1993, Monchanin seemed closer to me than Abhishiktananda, and the one whom God was calling me to imitate.

A few words about my own initiation: I was not raised a Catholic or in any other church. I followed the teachings of Paramahansa Yogananda, a yogi from Bengal who spent half his life in California and built a temple in Hollywood. I was fourteen when I read his *Autobiography of a Yogi*; it awakened strange longings in me and set the course my life would follow. In his book I found Bible passages I had never read before and the names of Catholic mystics whose writings I began to study. In my senior year at Occidental College in Los Angeles I converted to Catholicism and became a monk. I have worked on integrating Indian and Christian spirituality, but the real work has been on the level of my own humanity.

My search for God led me to pursue renunciation and integration as alternate tasks, corresponding with successive phases in my existence, but more and more I see them as interwoven in the fabric of my human and monastic vocation. Above all, I have come to see that while communities and institutions facilitate the accomplishment of these two tasks, they do so in an unclear way and with many compromises.

Formal initiation began in 1962, at the Hermitage of the Immaculate Heart of Mary, on the Big Sur coast in California, also called New Camaldoli. I joined the Church and the Camaldolese because I felt that only there could I practice what I had learned from Yogananda's books and from the Bhagavad Gita and the Upanishads — Hinduism's most sacred texts. Perhaps finding India by way of Hollywood, and Rome by way of India, was, for me, the shortest distance between two points.

The Italian superior and the American novice master of New Camaldoli trained me in a structured form of hermit life that had been transplanted from Tuscany to Big Sur in 1958. The Camaldolese monks in Italy and California follow the Rule of Saint Benedict, like the Trappists, the order Thomas Merton belonged to. But unlike a Trappist, who spends his day together with the monastic group — in other words, Trappists are strict cenobites — a monk in Big Sur lives in a small, separate cottage called a cell and spends most of his day imitating the desert hermits. At our American hermitage the emphasis was all on solitude and silence and the dark night of the soul. Saint John of the Cross was everyone's favorite mystic.

Yet the Camaldolese also belong to the Monastic Confederation presided over by the abbot primate of Sant'Anselmo — a monastery-university in Rome where the novices of New Camaldoli would eventually study theology, and where I stayed to teach. It was there that I met Bede Griffiths.

$\backsim$

Part I: 1984

$\backsim$

Shantivanam, July 18 – August 8

Wednesday, July 18

I visited northern India in 1978; this is my first time in the South. I hope to meet India as it really is, to see this country, its people, and its religions without taking anything for granted. I realize now that I was not ready to bear the full reality of India when I came here six years ago.

Now I am at Shantivanam, also called the Ashram of the Trinity, Saccidananda Ashram, and some of it is familiar to me from photographs, although it is simpler and more open and more Indian than I imagined.

Dom Bede was not here when I arrived (he was in Bangalore). Swami Amaldas was the only permanent community member present. He greeted me with both the Indian gesture (palms joined before the heart, called the namaskar) and the Italian greeting (a gentle hug). We met at Camaldoli on Dom Bede's first trip there. Amaldas asked if I would like some breakfast; I said yes, and he, still smiling, scolded me: "Why did you come by bus? If you had sent a telegram, we would have gone with a car to fetch you at the airport."

Thursday, July 19

My thatched-roof hut is under a banyan tree. A short distance away there are coconut palms and eucalyptus trees with the river Kaveri visible through them. One could get very romantic about this place. The weather is hot but breezy. Brief rain showers come and go, but it is not monsoon season yet, on this side of India.

In spite of jet lag — in this season there is a three and a half hour difference between Rome and India — I was up this morning when the first bell rang at five. At 5:15, all assembled in the dark temple for nama-japa, chanting of the holy Name: Om namah Khristaya — "Praise to Christ" — sung over and over to the melody Hindus use when chanting to Shiva. Mass was at 6:15,

8

after silent meditation. From the beginning, Monchanin had insisted (against Abhishiktananda's taste for Gregorian chant) on the priority of meditative practice over liturgical solemnity.

In the nineteen-fifties the liturgy was in Latin, and the adaptation of Christian rites to local cultures was hardly spoken of. The monks at Shantivanam now observe the dawn, noon, and sunset hours using a series of prayers borrowed from both Syrian and Roman liturgies, recited in English, with a Christian song or two in Tamil. The prayer begins with a chant in Sanskrit and a reading from the Vedic scriptures or from the local poets in classical Tamil. Different texts are recited according to different times of day, but they remain largely unchanged throughout the year, without regard to feasts or liturgical seasons. I find that this monotony contributes to the contemplative quality of the prayer.

This afternoon I walked out the painted gate in front of the ashram temple, with its three-faced figure representing the Trinity, and turned left down a rutted path to the river's edge. To my left was a plantain grove, and to my right was a stand of young eucalyptus trees, already very tall.

I looked out over the river's broad expanse and saw a palm-fringed shore more than a mile away. Up the river, looking west, I saw a bridge; beyond the bridge was a range of high hills and, veiled by the haze, the mountains of Coimbatore. To the east, the river spilled out over the horizon, and I could imagine I was looking out to sea, if I did not know that the Bay of Bengal was three hundred miles beyond.

"The ashram is noisy," some people told me. I suppose that for them the sounds of Indian life are noise. They are not so for me. I find the place utterly peaceful. So, except for an occasional peacock on the roof of my hut, shrieking its cry — this is a bit unnerving — the ashram is not noisy.

Shantivanam exhibits some of the characteristics of medieval hermitages, like Camaldoli. Compared to the grand abbeys like Cluny, the hermitages were much more informal and open. An abbey has to observe certain ritual niceties and stricter enclosure. A hermitage or an ashram may or may not observe them. Later history often turned this around, and hermitages were transformed into bastions of monastic conservatism and formality.

Saturday, July 21

Dawn sounds: birds exulting after a rainy night; the early train leaving for Trichy; distant music, soft, exotic.

This morning Dom Bede arrived from Bangalore and presided at Mass. After Mass, he greeted me with the Indian namaskar and bowing his head slightly, he gave me a restrained embrace.

"So you've arrived," he said. "We must have a good talk. Come along after coffee this morning." I came to his hut, and we sat on the porch. First he inquired about two Indian brothers, Christudas and Antonisamy, who are studying at Camaldoli. Then he asked whether I would be staying until December, when there will be a symposium here on contemporary science and religion. The biologist Rupert Sheldrake, author of *A New Science of Life*, will be present. I expressed my interest in taking part in the conference, but I thought: I shall have to see how well I adjust to the food and the climate.

At Mass, Bede uses the compromise 'Indian rite' — the limited ritual adaptation that the bishops have permitted. The priest says all the prescribed prayers of the Roman Missal, but he and the other participants sit yoga-style on the floor. Concelebrating priests drape an orange-colored shawl around their shoulders in lieu of a stole and chasuble. The preparation of bread and wine at the offertory is embellished by the 'sacrifice of the elements' — water, earth (flowers), air (incense), and fire, as in the Hindu rites of puja.

On Sundays, Mass begins a little later (around 6:45), and by seven the temple is filled with local villagers. The sung parts of the liturgy are in Tamil, and on Sunday the scripture readings are also in this language, which has a rich literary heritage. The sermon and most of the recited prayers are in English. The use of English is not just a concession to Dom Bede or Western guests but a necessity for visiting Indians who speak another of India's fourteen official languages and innumerable dialects.

I do not know to what extent the inculturation of Christian faith and monastic life in India will require de-Westernization. Certainly, the life and worship of the clergy and religious orders in this country are generally Westernized, but ritual adaptation alone is hardly more than window dressing. The life at Yogananda's monastic center in California was more Indian (at least as I remember it, back in the late fifties) than that in many convents and seminaries here.

Maybe inculturation is only one element, not even the principal one, in the general merging of cultural horizons and in the birth of a global consciousness. We have to find the grace of Jesus at the center of humanity's spiritual consciousness, as it emerges in a new millennium.

Monday, July 23

Dom Bede has been invited to visit a Tibetan monastery, called Sera Mei, in the hills outside Bangalore; he asked me to come along. While he is with the Tibetans, I shall stay at Asirvanam Benedictine Monastery near the city.

Yesterday, Bede, Amaldas and I walked along the river to a four-acre field that the ashram bought last year and on which they plan to build a hut for Dom Bede. They have planted millet, peanuts, and coconut palms.

On the way back, we visited a small Hindu temple dedicated to Murugan, the Boy-God, who is very popular in these parts. Some of the images inside were similar to the worst Catholic kitsch, but a painting of Murugan in the arms of his mother looked, for all the world, like a Byzantine Madonna.

Later, I went to see Sister Marie-Louise Coutinha at Ananda Ashram, which is opposite Shantivanam on the footpath leading to the river. Marie-Louise is from Mangalore and has belonged to a Franciscan missionary congregation for many years. She has lived in France, and she injects an occasional 'bon' or 'tiens' into her English. We had a good conversation about the situation of the church in India. Her assessment is balanced and just, in my opinion. She alluded in passing to her desire to affiliate with our Camaldolese nuns in Rome.

She told me that the hut I am in is where Dom Le Saux (Abhishiktananda) lived.

Friday, July 27

Dom Bede loaned me Abhishiktananda's essay on sannyasa.[2] 'Integral renunciation' is a key term for Abhishiktananda. He is not talking about a supposed synthesis of sannyasa and yoga (renunciation and integration) but about the total response to an instinct that dwells deep in the human heart and is already there before any specific religious expression arises. All such religious expressions — dharmas — give voice to this instinct, and those whom Hindus call sannyasis, Buddhists call bhikkhus, and Christians call monks or nuns, are simply persons who have ears attuned to the voice that sounds within them.

There is even a sort of 'monastic order' that includes them all. Monastics of whatever obedience recognize one another as brothers and sisters, across the borders of their respective dharmas, in their common witness to a reality that lies beyond all 'signs'. This 'universal monasticism' is obviously not an organization or a system of rules — reducing monasticism to organizations and rules, he says, ruins the true charism of monastic life, which consists in a thirst for the Absolute that is constantly felt and can never be quenched. Authentic monastics recognize their shared membership in this universal 'order' when they look into each other's eyes and see the depths where the Spirit works within them.[3]

Sunday, August 5

For the last two days, Dom Bede and Sister Marie-Louise have hosted forty people — clergy, religious, and lay — belonging to Satsangam, an organization devoted to helping young people in trouble here in India, mainly Westerners but also Indian youth. Bede gave the opening and closing talks.

I learned a number of things about Christianity in India, above all the extremely wide range of attitudes toward Indian culture itself. My observations about the general Westernization of Indian clergy and religious were confirmed.

The Charismatic Renewal is widespread among active Catholics in India, and all that can be said positively and negatively about this movement in the West is true here. Attitudes toward Indian religious traditions — sacred texts like the Upanishads and meditation practices like yoga and vipassana (Buddhist insight meditation) — range from indifference to hostility, with perhaps some lukewarm interest in between. Most charismatics are convinced that the study of Hindu writings and the practice of yoga are either useless or dangerous

Drugs are available and cheap, and this fact attracts foreign youths to places like Mumbai (formerly Bombay) and Goa. Drugs now circulate among Westernized Indian youth, who are about one fifth of the total adolescent population. Drug use is spreading rapidly through peer pressure and the desire to appear modern. Catholic schools are in no way immune to the plague of drugs.

An elderly British woman — not a member of Satsangam, but a guest of Marie-Louise — made a simple observation that I felt was one of the best insights of the past two days. She first came here in 1927, and she married a British army officer in Mumbai. One of the chief causes of India's current ills, she said, is the deculturizing effect of Western education, especially its pragmatic orientation — to get a better job and make more money. This was a matter of policy in colonial times, but it has continued without change after independence. No one seemed to pay much attention to what she said.

Bangalore, August 8 – 15

Wednesday, August 8
After evening nama-japa Dom Bede and I left by bullock cart for Kulittalai station, where we caught the night train to Bangalore. He will go visit the Tibetans, while I stay with the Benedictine monks at Asirvanam.

By the light of the three-quarter moon, we saw many children walking down the dirt road to the village for the late show at the cinema. Several of them quickened their pace to keep up with our cart. In Kulittalai, the streets were alive with people buying, selling and socializing, or simply being there.

How hard it is to fit life and living conditions here into my concepts of wealth and poverty! Is a household poor when there are no chairs or tables or beds but only mats, quilts, and pillows on the clean floor? Many families who could afford what we call furniture do not want it. Dom Bede said that some people keep their houses and shops primitive in order to avoid taxes.

Bede talks about the paradox of the cinema. India has an enormous motion picture industry. In Chennai alone, a new film comes out every day, many more in Mumbai. Kulittalai has its movie house, but nearly all the homes are without an indoor toilet — or an outhouse, for that matter — since one does everything by the canal or the river. Telephones and private autos are rare luxuries. Yet it seems as if the cinema were a part of ancient history like the prehistoric vehicle we are riding. You imagine that India has always been like this and will be so forever. But India is rapidly changing and losing its neolithic aura.

Friday, August 10
Our train reservations to Bangalore were in a 'three tier sleeper'. The 'berths' were wooden pallets without any concession to what

even an Indian would call comfort. I used my small bag as a pillow and tried to make the geometry of my body conform to the unyielding surface. So I rested a little — not as well, it seems, as Dom Bede, who was still sound asleep when I got up at six a.m.

We arrived in Bangalore at 8:30. We had a bun and some tea at a stand in the train station. Then we took an auto-rickshaw to Dharmaram College, where we had lunch.

Dharmaram College is a theological institute founded by Syrian-rite Carmelites. The graduate programs include courses in the Malabar liturgy and Hindu philosophy. On a wall in the college courtyard I discovered a large group photograph in which a tall, robed figure looked like a younger Dom Bede. I asked him whether it was he. "Yes," he replied, "I had just arrived in India, and I was present when they laid the cornerstone of the college. This was in 1955, and on that occasion I met Father Monchanin for the first time."

After lunch, a car and driver came to take Bede to the Tibetan monastery. I went to bed early, to make up for sleep lost on the train.

Bangalore is the fastest growing city in Asia. Situated on a high plateau, Bangalore's climate is generally cooler than at Shantivanam. Now is the season of rains in this part of the country, although the last two days have been mostly sunny.

After breakfast, I took a bus out to the village of Kengeri, near the monastery of Asirvanam. No one understood my request in English for directions — Asirvanam? Benedictine monastery? — until I said, "Catholic sannyasis?" Then they directed me to a road out of the village. Half an hour later I was at the monastery. The guest master welcomed me cordially and showed me to a room with adjoining bath — an Indian bath, of course (squat toilet, bucket and tin cup, cold water), but luxurious compared with the outhouse at Shantivanam.

Asirvanam was the first 'canonical' Benedictine community in India. Shantivanam was founded about the same time, but our ashram began informally and depended on charism for its validity, rather than ecclesiastical canons. Founded by Benedictines from Belgium, this monastery still has a decidedly European character. The monks, all but one of them Indian, celebrate the Hours of the Divine Office in English, using melodies adapted from Gregorian chant. Their robes are identical to those worn at their Belgian mother-house, although the color is a pale tan, not black. The community is numerous, about forty. Many must be novices, since they seem quite young.

Saturday morning, August 11
Let me paraphrase some thoughts from Abhishiktananda's *Initiation à la spiritualité des Upanishads*. Sannyasa can occur spontaneously, when one is driven by the Spirit to forsake all names and forms, even the name and form of a sannyasi. These are the avadhutas, 'drop-outs', the most uncompromising ascetics of all. He gives the example of Swami Ramdas, who initiated himself into sannyasa, putting on the orange robe after bathing in the Kaveri.[4]

Abhishiktananda tells the story of Ramana Maharshi, who at the age of sixteen left home and went straight up to Arunachala. A century before him, also in Tamil Nadu, Sadashiva Brahmendra abandoned his bride on their wedding day and later left his guru's ashram and spent the rest of his life wandering, naked and mute, up and down the banks of the Kaveri. Sannyasis, says Abhishiktananda, do not put on kavi robes to set themselves up as a special class apart from society, even though the robes have often been understood in this sense. Sannyasa transcends all classification, just as God transcends everything and cannot be reduced to any category. The ideal is God's own omnipresence — separate and beyond, yet at the same time present in everything, without any duality.[5]

An Indian historian, G. S. Ghurye, writes: "Two or three ascetics living together or moving together demonstrate that the ascetic ideal of complete withdrawal is already partially defeated. They begin to find some kind of habitation necessary. This habitation forms a monastic center. There emerge rules to regulate life at the center. Monastic life leads to the endeavor of creating social organization peculiarly fitted for the ascetic life. Thus, asceticism leading in its growth to monastic life creates the paradoxical phenomenon of social organization for those who not only negatived [sic] but also renounced social connections and individual wants."[6]

In other words, as soon as you start building the monastery, the ascetic life is finished.

Irony aside, the key phrase in this paragraph is 'paradoxical phenomenon'. Christian monastic life is even more of a paradox, since the inner dynamic of life in Christ tends toward the interiorization of all forms of ascetical practice and their transformation into the works of love.

Saturday afternoon, August 11
Abhishiktananda complains about the demands that modern society places on the individual: these are becoming even more stringent than those of primitive tribes, when individuality could barely be distinguished from the collective group consciousness. Even the churches and the world religions see the individual in terms of their own claims, and often go so far as to condemn the freedom of those who walk within their world without being a part of it.[7]

Sunday, August 12
What does it mean to be a monk, a Christian, a priest, in other words, to 'belong'? I do not belong to myself. I am nothing apart from God. God guarantees my ultimate individuality in a way that society, even the Church, cannot. "By the grace of God I am what I am," says St. Paul. The recognition of this is the greatest act of humility and, at the same time, the greatest act of

self-affirmation.

Even the Catholic priesthood assumes a different aspect in the light of sannyasa. I not only offer bread and wine — I am bread and wine. I vanish like the substance of the species, becoming the substance of the one sacrificial Victim, and what I am can no longer be seen, except by faith.

"Which way must I turn to address God? In what recess of my soul, in what point in space am I to sit, there to contemplate, supplicate, adore God? Wherever I go, God is already there. Whenever I try to say, 'I am,' God's 'I am' already shines deep within me and annihilates my 'I am' with its bright fire." (words of Sadashiva Brahmendra, quoted by Abhishiktananda.)[8]

The sannyasi's only witness, says Abhishiktananda, is to the mystery of Brahman — the Self of the human self. The prayer of the sannyasi is the silent experience of Fullness; it is the Word that comes forth from silence and draws the sannyasi back into silence.[9]

Abhishiktananda quotes the words of Christ — "The wind/Spirit blows where it wills" (John 3:8) — and applies it to the renunciant who has attained the paradoxical summit of renunciation, when there is no difference between wearing robes or not wearing them, living in a jungle or in a city, speaking or remaining mute, doing good works or doing nothing at all. The sannyasi, whose world is Spirit, lives free in this visible world.[10]

For Abhishiktananda, there is no limit to the paradox of 'renunciation' — the ultimate renunciation is to make a clean break with sannyasa itself or at least with whatever you can think or say about it. This final renunciation is what guarantees the authenticity of outward sannyasa.[11]

Monday morning, August 13
After a distracted meditation, I came to the following conclusion: a monastic vocation often runs counter to a person's purely natural inclinations. Here I am, an intensely private individual, a

natural loner, and I belong to a monastic order with a reputation for its hermits. My work as a writer keeps me by myself most of the day, even when other monks may be doing work in common. Yet I know in the depths of my being that unless I go against the grain of my all-too-natural hermit tendencies, I am failing precisely as a monk.

Can I say something positive about my being a monk? Maybe this: it leads me to the realization that the Father, who eternally begets a Son, has also conceived me in the womb of a world-mothering Spirit. In the beauty of my human conception, I discover a revelation of the reality that is in me and has neither beginning nor end. When I realize my eternal birth in the Son, I see that my task is to become flesh and dwell among my fellow humans in the freedom of Spirit.

Monday afternoon, August 13

The guest master came to my room to talk. He is the only monk here born in this state of Karnataka — all the others have family roots in either Kerala or Tamil Nadu. He told me that the community began in Tamil Nadu; the founders were of a mind to follow the ideas of Monchanin but, wishing to receive canonical status in the Church, they adopted the European model of monastic life. He personally feels there ought to be more inculturation, but most Indian Catholics are not ready for it and do not want their priests and religious to resemble Hindus in any way. He has been on retreat at Shantivanam and enjoyed the contemplative atmosphere he found there.

Asirvanam is near the place where Bede Griffiths, together with an Indian priest, Benedict Alapatt, lived during his first two years in India.

Tuesday, August 14

On the train back to Kulittalai, a young man in his early twenties, seeing Dom Bede in his orange robes, came over to talk to us. He belongs to a wealthy Kerala family, was raised a Catholic, and lives in a suburb of Bangalore. He said he wasn't very religious until he started to take part in a Charismatic Renewal group. He spoke to us especially about drugs. In the cities you can get whatever you want: marijuana and everything else, including heroin. In the biggest Catholic school in Bangalore, at least half the kids, he said, try smoking ganj, the local hemp, or taking pills, and they can get the stuff on the street in front of the school.

Shantivanam, August 15 – September 9

Wednesday morning, August 15
Dom Bede and I arrived back in Kulittalai at four this morning. We started walking to the ashram and met the bullock cart part way down the road.

August 15 is the feast of the Assumption of Mary for Catholics, but for India it is Independence Day. After Mass, Bede led the flag-raising ceremony, with a special Indian touch. The flag was folded into a bundle; after raising it, he gave a tug on the rope, the flag unfurled, and a shower of flower petals descended upon us.

Wednesday evening, August 15
In his evening talks, Bede often repeats what he has said in his books. The theology of Bede Griffiths comes out of his reading Thomas Aquinas in a Benedictine monastery — medieval thought coupled with a liturgical and contemplative spirituality. I doubt his hearers perceive the roots of Bede's thought, firmly planted in the soil of Catholic tradition and mysticism and in the monastic and other literature that he quotes explicitly or implicitly in his talks and writings.

Perhaps he transmits truths and insights to his listeners not primarily through his words and the concepts they articulate, but through his entire person, which is in perfect harmony with what he says. In fact, his person speaks louder than his words (which are sometimes inaudible, given the softness of his voice).

Dom Bede possesses the charism with which Hindus believe their gurus are endowed, that of 'giving darshan'. Darshan means 'seeing'; Hindus will say, "Let us go take darshan from Swami So-and-so." Seeing a genuine guru, one sees the divine. Worship offered to a holy person is referred immediately and, for educated Hindus, consciously to Brahman, the Absolute, and not to this particular human individual.

Authentic masters teach primarily by their silence and physical presence. A potential disciple finds someone he or she regards as a guru, pays homage and promises obedience, but does not immediately expect to be instructed in anything, not even meditation. Disciples have the duty and privilege of 'hewing wood and hauling water', while living in the guru's presence. Seeing a realized master for a long time is the way authentic disciples learn all they need to know about virtues and meditation practice. The climate of a gurukula (literally, 'family of the guru') is not that of a lecture hall or laboratory. Metaphorically, a disciple may be called an 'apprentice', but in a guru's workshop the craft is something that cannot be taught, only experienced directly.

The villagers, of whatever faith (the majority are Hindus), feel themselves blessed and instructed when they see Dom Bede, even when they do not understand a word he says.

Thursday morning, August 16
My meditation this morning took an almost Buddhist turn: perceiving the nothingness of creatures I enter into the No-Thing, God. I stand between two kinds of emptiness: the emptiness of creatures with regard to God, and the emptiness of God with regard to creatures.

I sense a positive meaning in the mystics' talk about 'emptiness' and 'annihilating the ego'. Emptiness is expectancy, like that of a chick with open beak waiting for its mother to feed it. Annihilation is abandonment, surrender. In my case, annihilating the ego means giving up caring about what people think of me and whether or not I look like their abstract idea of a monk. In a way, sannyasa should mean that I'm through with 'religion'. I could put this in a better way: it means the abolition of my religious ego and of the need for the security I used to find in being 'religious'.

Thursday afternoon, August 16
Indian people are not, by nature, contemplative. They generally live close to nature, and this is a good preparation for one kind of contemplation — the vision of the sacred Absolute in all natural phenomena. But Indians are characteristically active, restless, and incapable of remaining still and doing nothing. They become contemplatives by acting radically against their natural inclination. The sannyasi (the renunciant) becomes acosmic (one for whom the world simply does not exist), and the yogi strives to keep senses, mind, and intellect fixed in immobile one-pointedness.

There is another way, perhaps more truly Indian than the sannyasi's acosmicism; this is the Tantric way, the 'yoga of the heart', in which activity is transformed by doing one's work without seeking success or results, and in which meditation is not fixity but flow and vibration.

Friday, August 17
We have set August 22 as the date of my initiation into sannyasa. This morning I went to Trichy to buy some saffron-colored cloth, and now I am on retreat in silence.

Westerners have lost awareness of the effect of clothing or the lack of it on the human psyche. Indians are not very conscious of it either; at least it seems they do not realize what the general adoption of Western dress is doing to their culture and social relations. Almost no one is wearing the kurta any more. The young man on the train from Bangalore said that you do not get served in the cities if you walk into an office or a store wearing anything but a Western shirt and pants or, in some contexts, a business suit.

Psychologically, putting on the sannyasi's saffron cloth is like stripping bare. Having put on kavi, the renunciant will never again wear the covering of appearances, which are cast off forever.

Abhishiktananda said that a person's identity is grounded in his or her interiority and transcendence. To call myself a Catholic or a monk or even a religious person is true only to the extent that it corresponds to my interiority, that is, to something hidden and mysterious and inexpressible. External belonging, by itself, is not identity, and the identity can be there without the external belonging.

Sunday, August 19

The rite of initiation into sannyasa emphasizes renunciation in the most literal and radical sense. This emphasis is in harmony with Advaita-Vedanta — the philosophy of strict non-dualism. The sannyasi, who is also an advaitin, renounces all for the sake of the One. You find nothing ambiguous here, no paradox. But when Abhishiktananda pushes renunciation to the extreme of renouncing even renunciation, he ultimately arrives at paradox, the coincidence of opposites.

Tantrism takes a different approach and speaks of simultaneously 'renouncing all things and embracing all things.' Here I find myself more at home. Perhaps every monastic, of whatever tradition, must begin as an advaitin but mature as a tantrist.

The sannyasi renounces all and seeks to live in the void without despair. For me, sannyasa means that I am willing to have absolutely nothing and to receive every good thing as an absolutely free and unexpected gift. The paradox of poverty is that it creates an infinite capacity to receive and be filled.

Tuesday afternoon, August 21

The day before the initiation, with three other guests, I made a pilgrimage to the Rock of Ayermalai — a Shiva temple set on a cone-shaped hill that rises starkly out of the plain about ten kilometers from the ashram.

After Mass, we walked through the village and out into the countryside, shining green with paddy. After half an hour on the path we saw the Rock. It was an extraordinary sight, reddish-brown in color, its shape almost perfectly conical.

Two hours later, we came to the village that rings the foot of the hill, dominated by the temple, other buildings and porticoes of indeterminate age, and a huge tank (in India a 'tank' is a rectangular water reservoir used for ritual bathing and the washing of clothes).

We began the ascent, walking across a natural stone pavement in whose surface thousands of pilgrims have engraved the outline of their bare feet. The well-built steps that ascend the side of the rock pass through seven porches representing the seven chakras or centers of consciousness in the yogi's 'subtle body'. We stopped to rest under the one that corresponds to the manipura — the navel chakra. A priest with his water vessel, passing by on the way down, noticed our sandals and told us to take them off. We hid them under a bush and continued the climb barefoot. I wondered whether the live coals of the Tamil fire-walking ceremony could be hotter than those stone steps under the sun at noon. This was a tapas (penance) of the 'three fires': the sun above, the stone under our feet, and the fire of manipura lit by our fasting.

Entering the temple at the summit, we moved in a clockwise direction through corridors and colonnaded chambers like the shell of a nautilus. The first hall was dark and mysterious, with small, obscure images along a side wall. The growling of a monkey echoed against the ceiling. At the center, a slender brass column on a lotus-flower base extended up through a skylight, its top reaching for the heavens. This is skhamba — the world-axis and the support of the universe.

As we proceeded through an upward-sloping corridor, we heard a large bell ring in the distance, like the Angelus bell of a Christian monastery.

The first important shrine was a bas-relief of Shiva Dakshinamurti, where Shiva, 'the Benign', sits in meditation — a smile on his lips and his eyes closed — and gestures with the open palm of his right hand — the gesture of a master who teaches in silence.

After several more corridors, we came to a windowless chamber that encloses the lingam — a small, squat pillar broken at its summit, hence the legend of a king who had desecrated it. We stood at the entrance, and a young priest uttered a prayer before the lingam, honoring it with a camphor flame in a dish; he offered us ashes from the dish to place on our foreheads in three horizontal stripes, signifying the three saktis or energies of Shiva: will, knowledge, and action.

Leaving the shrine, we descended by another way that continued in the same clockwise direction. We sat on a shaded porch outside, waiting for clouds to shield the sun and cool the steps for our descent.

Tuesday evening, August 21
Let me try to say something about the tremendous emotion that swept over me like a great wave when I entered the first hall of the temple. I may have been reacting to the sinister growling of the monkey, but I was overwhelmed by a sense of an alien presence and of enormous psychic power in the place. I tried to concentrate on the symbolism of the skhamba and the great beauty of its form, piercing up into the light. But fear kept rushing up at me and with it the sense of having wandered into a different world, where I was definitely out of place and out of my depth.

When we came to the bas-relief statue of the teaching Shiva, I was strangely repelled by the smile. I mentally asked the image, "Who are you?" There was no answer.

At the lingam chamber, the odor of incense and oily smoke nauseated me. I did not put the ash on my forehead. I quickly went outside and leaned against a wall, watching the priests feed rice to the monkeys.

Was it just the fatigue and dizziness from the climb and my empty stomach?

I looked at the faces of the men and boys who live up here and serve Shiva. The priests were all brothers and cousins. Their features were sharp and their eyes intense, suggesting intelligence.

After two o'clock, we started down. At the village we drank tea and caught a bus for Kulittalai. On the way I spoke about my feelings in the temple to one of the Europeans who had come on pilgrimage with me. His reply was blunt: "Whatever your intellectual knowledge of Hinduism, you have obviously not come to terms with it emotionally."

He was right, but perhaps he experienced no disturbing emotions on the Rock of Ayermalai because he does not relate to Hinduism at all emotionally, as I do. The idealized vision of Hinduism that I absorbed from Yogananda's writings and from his monastic followers was an essential part of my adolescent search for religious truth. It colored not only my 'intellectual knowledge' of India's wisdom but also my personal religious sentiments. It continues to color my understanding of the Catholic faith.

I struggle with the meaning of sannyasa as moving beyond all outward religious signs. "Neither on this mountain nor in Jerusalem must you worship, but in Spirit and in truth," says Jesus.[12] The religion of the temple on Ayermalai is alien not because it is non-Christian, but because it is a religion of hereditary priesthood. A sannyasi is not a priest; a brahman who takes sannyasa renounces his priesthood. I remain a priest, but the meaning of my Christian priesthood bears only a tenuous analogy to that of the brahmans of Ayermalai. So I had no business in that temple, and in a way I have no business in any temple.

Wednesday, August 22

After morning nama-japa, Dom Bede led me down a path along the river to a spot more secluded than the watering place by the ashram. Ritually, everything went well. I felt no sweet emotions, nor did I really expect any. The sky was cloudy, and the rising sun was almost completely hidden. "Clouds and darkness are God's raiment," says a Psalm.[13]

During the ceremony a cloud passed between Bede and myself. I hesitated when I was to prostrate before him and stumbled over the words of the Jesus prayer ("Lord Jesus Christ, Son of God, have mercy on me a sinner"), which he had whispered into my ear as a mantra, the ritual formula that the guru transmits to the disciple. I saw in Bede's eyes a flash of anger, which lasted only a fraction of a second, replaced immediately by the gentleness and understanding that are the only light most people ever see in his gaze.

On the way back, Bede walked ahead of me, and in the light of the new sun I saw him treading on dry thorns, which pierced his bare feet. He strode on, seeming not to notice that he was bleeding. I was wearing sandals, and I carefully avoided stepping in the little puddles of blood that his feet left in the dust. I was very conscious of my unworthiness to walk in his footsteps.

At the end of the ceremony, I received a saffron dhoti and another saffron cloth to drape around my shoulders at prayer or when it is cool. I was given a Sanskrit name, Jyotirmayananda, which means 'he who finds joy in the One whose essence is light'.

Monday, August 27

Sannyasa is not the ceremony. It is not the robe or the Sanskrit name. I cannot say what my sannyasa initiation was, only what I hope it was and may become. Someone died and was reborn, emerging from the river's womb. The sannyasi, who reincarnates not one but many sannyasis of the past, has renounced the cycles of dying and rebirth. If I am in any sense a sannyasi, I have also renounced the river, and there is no compelling reason for me to stay here. India is neither here nor there. The one who went into the river died, and the river vanished.

Friday, August 31
I am still the Thomas I was, but now the meaning of my existence appears only in those moments when I am non-possessive and cause no fear in any creature.

I am beginning to sort out the feelings and thoughts that the pilgrimage to Ayermalai brought to the surface. The sense of being repulsed by the temple was similar to what I have felt, and sometimes still feel, about the externals of my own religion. There is in me, as I believe there must be in anyone who meditates, a special attraction to the imageless, the unstructured, and the non-ritual aspect of religion. Since becoming a Catholic and especially since entering the monastery, I have been forcing myself to conform to structures and to perform rituals correctly. I have even become something of a 'liturgist', against my better judgment and my deeper nature, although I do not think I have done so hypocritically.

Being a sannyasi does not mean that I have to reject liturgies or structures or laws. I probably will continue to be 'in them'; no longer am I 'of them'. I have been to the temple, but I am not to seek God there, or in the river. The one place of pilgrimage, say the Tantras, is the body of the yogi, and the one temple is the cave of the heart. My lingam, the sign of God, is the Body of Christ — Eucharist, my own body, the body of my neighbor. My liturgy is other people; le paradis, c'est les autres![14]

The best grace of sannyasa initiation has been self-knowledge and the ability to observe 'the war in my members' in a clear light.

Saturday, September 1
After reviewing what I wrote yesterday, I have to admit that my feelings this morning do not correspond very much with my convictions about sannyasa. I could describe my feelings using a Platonic-Stoic jargon, which once was common coin in Christian monasteries: "It is the burden of the flesh." I do not mean "the scourge of carnal lust" but the sense of my body as a dead weight, chained to the dead weight of other bodies — the body as tomb. Attached to this dead weight, like another shackle, is the obsessive thought of the monastic institution I belong to, its problems, and what I imagine to be the solutions to these problems. But the inner turmoil is bathed in the most clear, dispassionate, and uncompromising light. The light floods my soul and exposes the illusion that underlies thought, but it will take time for the feeling that accompanies thought to go away.

This clarity makes me uncomfortable, but it also inexplicably comforts me. At least I know that as long as I can see this mess and am willing to look straight at it, some good is being accomplished. The tomb, after all, is not my body but my ego. The ego is the dead weight, the 'Old Man'. But he must die, and, thank heaven, he is already close to death.

Saturday, September 8
From behind the dark cloud of thoughts, a light re-emerged last evening, and I realized the wonder of this gift of India, the wonder of my being here and belonging to it all.

The ashram has received many guests these last few days. A Jesuit from Belgium, now many years in India, spoke to me of Abhishiktananda, the voluble conversationalist, the agile mind, the body in constant motion. But did he see the still center of all that motion? Did he see Abhishiktananda the contemplative of divine darkness, the trinitarian advaitin?

A married couple from Italy, bewildered by a too-full schedule prepared for them by Caritas International, wish they could stay in the ashram longer to digest what they have seen. In particular, they have seen many missionary priests who work in terrible isolation and whose lives are spiritually desolate. They have seen overworked, burnt-out nuns. They have seen priests and bishops in India more Roman than bishops and priests in the Vatican.

A young school teacher with sad eyes, from a village at the foot of Mount Arunachala, told me her story. Her name is Rani. She was raised a Catholic and has always practiced her religion. Her grandfather, an illustrious and wealthy brahman, was converted to Christianity not by hearing sermons of missionaries but by reading English literature.

"Christianity is incomplete without the *Upanishads*," she said.

She discovered Hinduism through Dom Bede's *The Cosmic Revelation*, and then she read the *Upanishads*. "It was like reading a novel," she said, "and I couldn't put it down until I had finished it." She also reads the poetry of Wordsworth and Keats. She finds more spiritual meaning in them than in the Bible.

"The Bible, especially the Old Testament, is often confusing and contradictory," she said. "It is also too full of precepts and commandments. People do not like to be told what to do, but they will accept a spiritual ideal that is lived concretely. The Hindu gurus teach by example and by their poetry."

She has visited Ramana Maharshi's ashram at Arunachala and Sri Aurobindo's in Pondicherry. She desires to be a sannyasi, but everyone tells her that the only alternatives for an Indian Catholic woman are entering a convent or getting married.

Her words made me ponder a number of things: the dogmatic insistence on the Bible, especially since the Second Vatican Council; the difficulty of translating the language of the Bible into terms intelligible to Indians, who are heirs to a religious culture two thousand years older than the Bible; the lack of poetry and the excess of precept in the preaching of Christianity.

What is 'translation'? There are Bibles in Tamil and Hindi and even Sanskrit, but do they give a dynamic equivalent of biblical thought-patterns to those who speak India's languages? That is, do the church translations give Indian listeners and readers the same inner experience had by those who heard the prophets and the apostles? Christianity came to India in sub-apostolic times; yet, Catholics are only two percent of the population. Traditional preaching and teaching have proven ineffective even for preserving the piety of those raised in the closed caste of Syrian-rite Catholicism.

Sunday, September 9

"Christianity is seen here as charity, not as wisdom," said Dom Bede, commenting on the first verses of Colossians. "We need to discover Christian gnosis."

Dom Bede told us his favorite story about Jules Monchanin: "When Father Monchanin first arrived in Kulittalai, he asked a group of village children, 'Where is God?' The Christian children all pointed to the sky; the Hindus pointed to their hearts."

Bede added, "An Indian spontaneously sees God as all-pervading, Christ as all-pervading, the God-realized saint as all-pervading."

This is something more than the philosophical question of transcendence versus immanence. The Upanishads affirm transcendence when they proclaim Brahman as neti-neti, 'not this, not that'. Christianity also affirms immanence; when you have said, with Thomas Aquinas, "God is in everything by power, by presence, and by essence," what more can you say? The real problem for an Indian theology is sacramentality. Hindus and many Indian Christians find they have no concepts to deal with the affirmation of the real presence of the body of Christ in the Eucharist. He is all-pervading, isn't he? Then how can he be more there than here?

Bede spoke about the decay of India's spiritual culture, taking place paradoxically within a sociological revival of Hinduism and even of Hindu fanaticism. He said, "There was a brahman in Tannirpalli whose daughters used to perform classical Indian dances based on religious themes. Now all they want to do are the kinds of dances they see in the movies."

Tomorrow, I go to Trichy and spend the night at Saint Paul's Seminary, on the way to Arunachala and Ramana Maharshi's ashram.

Arunachala and Shantivanam, September 10 – 20

Monday evening, September 10
I arrived at dusk in Tiruvannamalai and took a cycle-rickshaw up to Ramana Maharshi's Ashram at the foot of Mount Arunachala. I was given a hut with an attached bath. After supper (rice, curry, and beets on a 'plate' of woven leaves), I tried to put into writing what I saw on the way here.

The bus headed inland from the coast through a rock-strewn landscape of low hills. The ancient rock formations seemed graven with some mysterious, solemn, and definitive message. The life of the goatherds in these fields is anything but idyllic, because this is a land for spiritual battles. The mountain of Arunachala is the Spirit's sign of victory. "I lift up my eyes to the hills; from where does my help come?" (Psalm 121:1).

To me, India appears apocalyptic, as if the spiritual destiny of the human race were to be decided here. I can believe that the Last Judgment will take place, not in Jerusalem, but at the source of the Ganges, or on Adam's Bridge between the southern tip of India and Sri Lanka, or on the mountain of Arunachala.

Tuesday, September 11
The ashramites are all brahmans. The elder brahmans and their students wear white robes, not saffron, although they observe the

sannyasi's rules of chastity and non-possession. "I am very devoted to Jesus," said the kindly brahman who showed me around the ashram. "I love him dearly, because he prayed for those who spat upon him and tortured him and nailed him to a cross. Jesus said, 'Forgive them, for they know not what they do,' and after three days he came back to these very men and showed himself to them. In the same way, Ramana Maharshi also practiced compassion toward those who mistreated him."

Ramana saw his soul as the 'I am' without a predicate nominative, without a name that tongue can utter. Perhaps he saw the image of the 'I am' who spoke to Moses.

The temples, centered on the tombs of Ramana and his mother, who became his disciple, are of recent construction but exquisite in their finely-crafted design and details. The worship of the holy man is clearly directed to the divinity without name or form that every educated Hindu regards as the one, true object of worship. Ramana became transparent to God, for himself and for others.

The tour ended in the old building where Ramana Maharshi once lived and presided silently at daily audiences. I sat in meditation there with another guest for half an hour.

Wednesday afternoon, September 12
In the main temple, worship is the chanting of Vedas and the clockwise circumambulation of Sri Ramana's tomb. I did not attend the service this morning but returned to the hall where Ramana 'gave darshan' to his devotees, and I meditated with a few other guests.

After breakfast I hiked up the mountain. The sun was warm, but the air and the rocks were still cool after last night's rain. One third of the way to the summit is the Skhanda Ashram, where Ramana lived as a hermit from 1915 to 1922. In the midst of an oasis of coconut palms and mangoes, there is a low structure with a terrace, built against the natural cavity of the rock, and a spring that provides a continual flow of water. Abhishiktananda also meditated there. From the mountain we saw the vast temple complex in town.

The mountain was what I really came to see. It spoke to me of God, but also of other mountains on this planet where I have sensed God's presence, like Shasta or the Tuscan Apennines or the Swiss Alps near Vinal.

Wednesday evening, September 12
Ramana Maharshi's life as an ascetic and contemplative began in his seventeenth year with a near-death experience achieved without physical trauma, through intense mental concentration on the contingency of his physical and psychic being. Having seen through the illusions of the skin-encapsulated ego, he left his home and hiked to the temple in the shadow of Mount Arunachala. Upon reaching the shrine, he entered the sanctuary, embraced the lingam, and cried, "My Father, my Father."

Clad only in a loin cloth, he persevered in meditation on the temple precincts, eating only if someone spontaneously offered him food. Later he retired to the cave, one-third of the way to the summit, where he remained for seven years. Disciples began to arrive, seeking his darshan, among them his mother and a few other relatives. Ramana never sought the sort of public following that even Yogananda, during his first decade in America, found and welcomed. There have been Western followers of Ramana, and a few have written books about him. Yogananda paid him generous homage in the *Autobiography of a Yogi*. Thirty-four years after his passing, Ramana Maharshi's legacy is this orderly ashram of brahmans, not much larger than Shantivanam, where there is nothing of the spectacular cult that surrounds latter-day gurus like Satya Sai Baba and Osho Rajneesh.

The ashram is filled with photographs of Ramana, most of them taken during the last decade of his life. He is almost always smiling; the smile is now benevolent, now infantile, now wry and ironic. His gaze is deep, gentle, and empty of that glint of shrewdness that I have seen in the eyes of some other gurus. Contemplating the photographs, I felt a gentle blessing.

Thursday morning, September 13
Monchanin made several visits here. In 1949 he and Le Saux spent a few days in Ramana's ashram, preparing for the official founding of Shantivanam, which took place in March of the following year.

Later, Abhishiktananda wrote of his impressions. His expectations were, he said, "fervent," and for this reason he was disappointed. The reverence and recollection of Ramana Maharshi's disciples impressed him more than the guru himself, who seemed benevolently indifferent to their devotion, rather like Abhishiktananda's own grandfather, as he remembered him. He could see no halo around the man. A fever, the following day, drove Abhishiktananda back to Shantivanam, pondering an English devotee's remark about the 'intellectual baggage' with which he was encumbered, and which had hindered his vision.

Lying ill at Shantivanam, Abhishiktananda realized that the meeting with Ramana Maharshi had, in fact, touched him at a depth beyond his own reach. Six months later, he returned to Arunachala, only to find the guru gravely ill. He was allowed to see him for only a few seconds, but the impression was more profound than he could describe. Abhishiktananda planned to make a longer retreat there in the spring of 1950, but two days before his departure he read of Ramana's death in a Tamil newspaper. "The Maharshi was no longer there," he wrote, "and any desire to return to Tiruvannamalai at once left me."

Thursday evening, September 13
I spent the afternoon sitting outdoors under a mango tree, looking at the mountain. Seeing the mountain, I kept seeing Ramana Maharshi's face, or rather, I felt as if I were merging with

him, seeing his face from within. The feeling was very hard to describe. Perhaps I was close to perceiving the reality of the absolute 'I am' in and beyond this 'I am'.

Abhishiktananda did return to Mount Arunachala after the death of Ramana Maharshi. He also discovered, as I have, the mountain as an icon of the Absolute. This mystery was, for Ramana and his fellow Hindus, personified as Shiva, India's primordial divinity, worshipped not as one of a pantheon but as the One itself, the Eternal, the 'Immobile Dawn' — as the word Arunachala may be translated.

Friday, September 14

Ramana taught through his silence and his visibility, but he did write a few pages in Tamil, and some disciples have transcribed interviews with him and published them.

"Solitude is in the mind," said Ramana Maharshi. "One might be in the thick of the world and yet maintain perfect serenity of mind; such a person is always in solitude. Another may stay in the forest, but still be unable to control his mind. He cannot be said to be in solitude. Solitude is an attitude of the mind; a man attached to the things of life cannot get solitude, wherever he may be. A detached man is always in solitude."

Ramana was what the Rig Veda calls a muni — an ascetic who practices both silence and nudity — in his case, mitigated by the loincloth he always wore. The occasional mitigations of his silence served to draw his listeners into constant meditation on the inner teaching of the Self, the Spirit. True silence, he said, is "that state which transcends speech and thought… Subjugation of the mind is meditation: deep meditation is eternal speech. Silence is ever-speaking; it is the perennial flow of 'language.' It is interrupted by speaking, for words obstruct this mute language. Lectures may entertain individuals for hours without improving them. Silence, on the other hand, is permanent and benefits the whole of humanity."

Saturday, September 15
I cut short the retreat at Arunachala in order to have a few more days at Shantivanam. I caught the night train to Trichy and was back at Shantivanam in time for breakfast. In little more than a week, I will go to visit the shrine of my patron saint, the Apostle Thomas, and then leave for Italy. I have received many blessings here, and I know that India will continue to draw me back.

India was an essential part of my culture when I was growing up in California, even though I viewed Yogananda's monastery and temple and yoga through lenses tinted with Western Christianity. The spiritual culture of India is still accessible to me in California and Italy, almost as much as it is here. After all, a person can absorb only so much.

Sunday, September 16
After midmorning coffee, I met with Dom Bede. I will need to have another long talk with him before I leave. Am I eager to get back to Italy and California? Am I reluctant to leave India? Perhaps both. However, it seems that God wants me to conclude this stay in India now, and to leave the door open for another, longer retreat.

Later I talked with Brother Mani, the one Indian member of the Little Brothers of Jesus. He is deeply committed to penetrating into the religious heart of India. We agreed that there are dimensions of Hinduism into which we can and must enter — its most universal dimensions. There are others into which we cannot enter, and perhaps they will always remain closed to us. Mani understood my feeling of being repulsed by the temple of Ayermalai.

Saint Thomas Mount, September 21 – 25

Friday evening, September 21
My last conversation with Bede touched on personal questions.

He gave me his blessing and invited me to return, not only for a retreat, but also to help with the formation of novices.

The train from Trichy arrived in Chennai this morning ten minutes ahead of schedule. I found the bus to the southern outskirts of town, and one of the passengers let me know when I reached my stop. From there I walked to Aikiya Alayam, the ashram of Jesuit Father Ignatius Hirudayam. I had a bath and rested in the small, cool room.

In the evening, I attended Hirudayam's Mass. The Indian gestures and other ritual adaptations were more elaborate than at Shantivanam, and it was all in Tamil. After Communion the four sisters attending sang a song.

Hirudayam is the very image of a South-Indian sage. With his long, white hair and beard, and typical Dravidian features, he resembles Sri Yukteswar, Yogananda's guru. Obviously a man of deep prayer, in his soft, brown eyes you often see a mischievous twinkle, the presage of a warm and innocent smile.

Saturday evening, September 22
The following afternoon I visited the basilica of Saint Thomas ('San Thome'). Oral tradition says that it was built on the site of a Jain temple and monastery. The local Jains also accept this tradition. A crypt beneath the main altar is the apostle's tomb, with a painting of him dressed in kavi like a Hindu sannyasi. In fact, all the icons of him that I have seen show him clothed in a saffron tunic with a reddish cloak over his shoulders. Like John the Evangelist, he has no beard, which perhaps means that he, too, remained celibate.

Sunday, September 23
The next day, I made pilgrimage to Saint Thomas Mount outside the city. The Portuguese built the present shrine; you could imagine you were in Brazil. As at Ayermalai, there is a stairway from the base of the hill, but not so steep and you are not required

to remove your sandals. Inside the shrine, an image of the Virgin and Child 'painted by Saint Luke' is obviously no earlier than the fourteenth century. The stone cross over the altar may be more ancient, perhaps a monument placed here by Syrian Christians, but it cannot be of apostolic times.

The real monument to the martyrdom of Thomas is the living memory of him among the people. They say that their apostle was slain on this hill with a lance, and I believe them.

I celebrated the Mass, whose gospel reading told me that I, a laborer of the eleventh hour, receive the same pay as those who have been working since sun-up. I heard these words: "If your sins be red as scarlet, I shall make them whiter than wool, says the Lord." Two Sisters, missionaries of Saint Francis, responded to the prayers, and after Mass an elderly Capuchin friar gave me three cups of sweet lime juice to refresh me. I walked down and caught the bus back to Aikiya Alayam.

After lunch and a nap I visited Kapaliswarar temple near the center of town, not far from San Thome basilica. It is a perfect miniature of the greater Dravidian temples. The principal gopuram (gate tower) is entirely polychrome, as were the temples in ancient times (the same was true of Greco-Roman cult statuary, art historians remind us). The profusion of images reflects the total sociality of India's people, who cannot conceive of not being together in all they do. A private, introspective, 'eremitical' American like me, feels overwhelmed by the crowd on the city street and the crowd carved in stone, until he remembers that Dante's heaven is crowded too. How much 'pagan', Greco-Roman myth lives on and is baptized in the Divine Comedy! The heaven carved in the gate of this temple is the ideal image of that which gives joy to this gentle, much-suffering people: their social life, their togetherness, their being "one body" with their divinities. Le paradis, c'est les autres!

Tuesday, September 25

After receiving Father Hirudayam's blessing, I left for the airport. Chennai is a wonderful city, my favorite in India. Probably, what appeals to me most is the village atmosphere you still feel here, in spite of urban sprawl. But Mumbai is beautiful too, in its own way, even the shacks of coco-matting along the road to the airport. These are inhuman living conditions; yet in the light of oil lamps and of the sheer human presence, a grace shines forth, like a prophecy that, in time, this people of God will be set free and regain their full human dignity.

I have incurred another debt to India on this trip, in addition to the long-standing debt to the India I learned to love by reading Yogananda's autobiography, the India that showed me the contemplative path. Perhaps what I have written here will be a first payment.

Part II: 1988 – 1989

Four years passed between my first stay at Shantivanam and a series of retreats there during the last five years of Bede Griffiths' life. I saw him once again in Big Sur before I returned to Camaldoli in the Tuscan Apennines. In 1987, a Christian lay community invited me to take part in organizing an international congress in Assisi on dialogue among Hindus, Buddhists, and Christians. Founded in the nineteen-thirties by a saintly priest, Giovanni Rossi, the community is dedicated to bringing a progressive view of Catholicism into the Church and the market-place. Some of its members, called 'volunteers', bind themselves by a private commitment to celibacy, without seeking canonical status in the Church. Their community is popularly known as 'The Citadel' (la Cittadella di Assisi), from the name of the conference center and publishing house they established in the town of Saint Francis. In recent years they have intensified their involvement in interfaith dialogue, even to the extent of risking censure from the local bishop and the Vatican.

After the congress, the Cittadella asked me to guide some of the participants on pilgrimage to Buddhist shrines. In August 1988 we traveled to Nepal and northern India. After the tour I made a brief retreat at Shantivanam, before returning to Italy and taking part in another congress organized by my friends in Assisi. The Cittadella invited me to accompany another group to southern India and Sri Lanka the following summer.

Nepal, Bodhgaya, Sarnath, July 25 – August 8, 1988

Monday, July 25
Every departure is a risk, even apart from the congestion of the skies. As a believer, I appreciate the symbolic resonance of taking off, of separating from the earth; but as a man of little faith, I find myself fearful like Peter when he tried walking on water. I am with a group of people who have their own preoccupations, unwillingness to risk, and littleness of faith. My task will be to

help them approach India and Nepal without fear and with the prudent innocence of the gospel — in the words of Jesus, as "serpents and doves."

At 12:05 p.m. we took off over the Mediterranean on a two-hour flight to Istanbul. The long layover there may give us time to visit the city.

Announcements were made in Turkish. Out the window I saw the delicate blue of the water, a white haze on the horizon, and the vague silhouettes of islands, probably Capri and Ischia. The plane circled the islands moving east; I saw cloud-capped mountains to my left: the Southern Apennines. Then we were over land again: Basilicata and Apulia. Out over the water, the plane banked to starboard and skirted the south of Greece.

On arrival at Istanbul we were herded into the transit lounge and left there like cattle in a holding pen. But the Cittadella volunteer in charge of our group made the right kind of requests to the right people, and we were let out to take taxis into town. We went to the ancient Christian basilica of Hagia Sophia, but found it closed. We crossed the square and entered the Blue Mosque after evening prayers; the Muslims built the mosque as a twin to the basilica. Inside the mosque, light entering through the floral patterns of stained-glass windows bathed the blue-green Majolica tiles. Within the central nave, a few men were still at their devotions, sitting and prostrating beneath the pulpit; behind us some women did the same.

I have with me a book on Islamic mysticism, to fill the gaps in my knowledge of India, where the Muslim Mughals once had a great empire. Islam in India represents, for number of adherents, the largest Muslim population of any non-Islamic country in the world: fifteen per cent of India's nine hundred million inhabitants.

Tuesday evening, July 26
The Istanbul-Delhi flight landed at the new Indira Gandhi

Airport; you could mistake it for a terminal at Heathrow or JFK. The bus from Swagatam Tours and Travels took us, suitably garlanded, to the Kanisha Hotel. The main lobby had frescoes representing India's various religions — the 'OM' symbol of Hinduism, the Buddhist creed, the Madonna and Child — on the domed ceiling. My room had a view of parks and a busy intersection.

After lunch we toured the city. First stop: Humayun's tomb, called 'the little Taj Mahal', in Delhi's dominant red sandstone with white and black marble inlay. From the terrace, we saw a Sikh temple — center of worship for Panjabis resident in the capital.

Then we went to the shrine of Mahatma Gandhi — a moving experience, the perfect beginning of a visit to India. In the center of a park, where the Mahatma was cremated, is his samadhi — a massive block of polished, black granite, inlaid in brass with his last words (in Hindi): "He Ram," meaning, "O God!" Samadhi means 'meditation' or 'contemplative ecstasy', but metaphorically it refers to the great meditation of death and hence to a holy person's tomb. An elaborate design in flower petals adorned the surface of the shrine. I told my companions that the only memorial to Gandhi outside India is at Paramahansa Yogananda's Lake Shrine near Hollywood; it contains a small portion of Gandhi's ashes, given to Yogananda by India's ambassador to the United States.

Leaving the Gandhi memorial, the bus took us directly to the big Jahan Mosque just before evening prayer. It was closing to non-Muslims, but we were allowed to step into the outer court, until the muezzin started his chant. We ended the afternoon at a high-class souvenir emporium, with a snake charmer (two small and two large cobras).

The guide from Swagatam Tours, an Indian woman who spoke Italian, asked me where I am going after the tour, all about the ashram, about not marrying (sannyasa), and not being allowed to love a woman, et cetera.

Wednesday morning, July 27
A gift of psychic India during this morning's meditation: I saw a luminous om (the Sanskrit character) floating in golden light above a lotus flower; surrounding the lotus were female figures, personified saktis (energies).

I thought about the questions the Indian tour guide asked me on the bus yesterday. There is no simple answer, but what really answers such questions is the way I say whatever I say, the implicit message underlying my explicit statement.

Trying to convince anyone about celibacy with rational arguments always comes across as an effort to convince myself. People will perceive evasive answers as insincere, if not entirely phony.

Thursday, July 28
In the afternoon, we flew to Nepal. The next day, as I lay sick in the bed of a hotel room in Katmandu, I puzzled over a strange sense of time compression; twenty-four hours spent in this bed seemed like a week. Some microbe I carried here from India (from a bad egg or a piece of unwashed fruit) sent me down with fever and vomiting. Although I still had a headache, the fever was gone, thanks to sulfa medicines and sleeping all night and most of the morning.

While I stayed behind, the group went to Patan, where the Jesuits have an elite school and the only Catholic Church in Nepal. Tomorrow I hope to visit temples with the four or five others who got sick like me. I will be seeing the temples for the second time: I was here in 1978 with two Italian priests, and the shrines engraved themselves deep in my memory.

Friday evening, July 29
Nearly the whole group came with me to Bodh-nath Stupa, in

Katmandu's Chinatown. It was founded by a Tibetan woman and is served by lamas (Tibetan Buddhist monks). We walked clockwise around the stupa — an enormous dome whose painted eyes at the summit looked down on us implacably. Then we drove out of town to an ancient river temple, dedicated to Pashupatinath, Shiva as divine shepherd. I explained Shiva and the lingam and yoni to the group, and then withdrew to sit on the non-Hindu side of the river, remembering my pilgrimage here in 1978. With the little ones of this Hindu Nineveh, I meditated on Shiva (the 'benign'), who sometimes manifests as Bhairava (the 'terrible' aspect of God).

After supper, a professor of anthropology at Katmandu University, Dipak Raj Pant, gave us a talk on Nepal's religions. I met Dipak in 1981. Italian missionaries had brought him over to study philosophy at the Gregorian University in Rome. He has just published his dissertation on the symbolism of masks, and speaks perfect Italian. Dipak belongs to the highest caste of brahmans; his father gave him a Life of Christ in Nepalese, telling him to study all religions with the same reverence as he studied his own.

His exposition of Hinduism — 'an anarchic religion' — and Buddhism — 'the best of Hinduism' — was absolutely brilliant. I fully agreed with his setting the two traditions side by side, illumining the one with the other. Dipak said he may not be able to remain in Nepal; he finds himself at odds with conservative elements in the political and academic establishment, in spite of his not feeling any urge to start a revolution.

Sunday, July 31

Saturday morning we were up at four, and by 5:15 a.m. twenty of the twenty-five tour members were on a bus to Lumbini, birthplace of Gautama Sakyamuni, the Buddha. Lumbini is down in the plain but within Nepalese territory. Arriving at the guest lodge in Lumbini that evening, sweaty and tired, we found eight not-very-clean rooms with three or four beds in each. All took the accommodations in good spirit. In the wee hours monkeys howled, sounding like coyotes, and at four the crows began loudly chanting their sutras. I was the only one up at that hour and got to use the toilet and shower on the other side of the courtyard.

Last evening I gave the group a stupid dharma talk, with confusing answers to a lot of good, open questions. For many, the great preoccupation was hell and reincarnation. They seemed reassured, if not entirely convinced, by my answers.

This morning we had a good meditation together, before touring the Buddha's natal site. Although UNESCO has apportioned funds for the building of an international conference center here, only a part of the archeological remains have been excavated. In the third century BCE, the Emperor Ashoka marked the site of the Buddha's birth with a column, engraved with an edict promoting devotion to the Enlightened One. A small pond nearby was in all likelihood the temple 'tank' (pool for ablutions), where he was washed at birth. We met monks on the grounds, one from Burma, another from China. The Burmese monk showed us architectural drawings of the center that is to be built here, with Western-standard hotels.

Tuesday, August 2
On the way back to Katmandu I gave a better talk. Buddhism marks its newness with respect to Hinduism by the religious value it attributes to the community, the sangha, into which one enters not through birth but through choice. While family, caste, and the society based on them are sacred for Hinduism, liberation from spiritual bondage requires that one leave these structures. The hermit, the sannyasi, freed from caste and family responsibilities, is a sign of the Absolute for those still bound to them, but he does not form the seed of a new society; no spiritual community gathers around him. One or a few disciples with a guru constitute

the gurukula, but this is not a community. In his autobiography, Yogananda mentions a few young men present in Sri Yukteswar's hermitage during the years of his own discipleship, but there was no lasting brotherhood among them.

Community is essential to Christianity: "Unus christianus, nullus christianus." ("A Christian by herself/himself is no real Christian," variously attributed to Tertullian, Saint Cyprian of Carthage, and Saint Augustine.) Something similar can be said of Buddhism, which cannot exist without a sangha. Even though this community is limited to those who have put on monastic robes, it is one of the 'three gems' of a lay Buddhist's profession of refuge: "I take refuge in the Buddha, I take refuge in the Truth, I take refuge in the Community."

Friday, August 5
The following day the group split up; some went trekking in the Himalayan foothills, while I and the others visited the hilltop shrine of Swayambhu-nath.

I hardly remembered the view of the valley surrounding the temple hill from my pilgrimage here in 1978. This time it affected me deeply, with a sense of the social function of a religious center that is openly and innocently syncretistic. You almost never hear 'syncretism' used in a positive sense, but here the mixing of Buddhist and Hindu worship seemed perfectly natural, even inevitable. Historically the two traditions never severed ties, in the way that the Christian Church separated itself from Judaism. I once heard an elder Buddhist monk from Sri Lanka use the expression 'sister religions' to explain the relationship between Hinduism and Buddhism, comparing them to Catholic and Protestant Christianity.

Ascending the hill, we came to a medium-sized stupa surrounded by four smaller ones, and for a moment I thought this was the main shrine. But another flight of steps led us to the real stupa, only slightly smaller than Bodh-nath, with an even more impressive gilded and eyed tower on top. Other shrines and temples dotted the compound. Curio shops surrounded them, and side alleys led to housing for the priestly families who serve here. I thought of Assisi and similar hill-towns in Italy, with their castles and basilicas. In spite of the anarchic juxtaposition of rites and devotions, the spiritual atmosphere was harmonious. Bells rang and sutras resonated from loudspeakers, but a veil of silence seemed to cover the hill.

There were several newly-built monasteries on the hill. We entered one of them as lamas chanted mid-day sutras with drums and cymbals. A monk smiled his welcome, when he saw us come in and sit reverently on the floor to listen. Then he took us to a hall where students and teachers sat in rows facing each other. Each of the monks was reading his own book out loud; it sounded a bit like a contest. Two students engaged in a loud debate with broad gestures, clapping hands and snapping fingers. I observed the slightly amused faces of the elders; the students, on the contrary, looked absolutely serious.

Sunday, August 7
Our pilgrimage to Bodhgaya in India, the place of Gautama Sakyamuni's enlightenment, coincided with the feast of the Transfiguration of Christ, August 6.

Gaya is just off the Great Trunk Road, half-way between Delhi and Calcutta. Paddy fields along the highway were intensely green from this year's abundant rains. Seen out of the corner of your eye, the fields, bordered with palms, could be mistaken for a golf course (like the golf course adjoining the international air terminal at Katmandu). Such comparisons aside, India in this season has all the attributes of an earthly paradise.

Green hills, dotted with enormous, black boulders, lined the last stretch of the road approaching Gaya. On the Great Trunk Road tourists are rare; children in one of the villages along the way lined up by the road to jeer at these strangers, traveling in their bus to places where they do not belong.

This ancient temple town, now sacred to the memory of the Buddha, is not on the tourist map. I saw no other Westerners there. The buildings, rebuilt a century ago by General Cunningham from the rubble left by seventeenth-century Mughal iconoclasts, are impressive, but the main attraction is the great Bo tree, a fourth-generation descendant of the original, under which Sakyamuni sat and attained his awakening. Seeing there was no appropriate place to meditate under the tree, we sat for a few minutes in a tower of the main temple; this brief meditation was the high point of the visit.

The sequence of events in the Buddha story is identified with a series of stages in a short walking pilgrimage through the town. After six years fasting on the side of the river opposite Gaya, he broke his fast — to the scandal of his five disciples — by taking a bowl of rice gruel offered to him by the noblewoman Sujata. After the disciples left him and went to Sarnath, he crossed the river. There, on a full moon night, he sat himself under the spreading ficus religiosa and became the awakened Buddha. For seven weeks he continued his meditation, walking and sitting at seven different places near the tree. At one of them the god Brahma appeared and begged him, for the sake of the entire universe, not to go straight into Nirvana but to remain on earth and show the way to suffering beings.

We spent the night in the Thai guest house (each Buddhist country has a monastery here). My sleep was short, and I used the wakefulness to meditate, grateful for the remembrance of the Buddha that, in a moment of temptation many years ago, saved my soul.

I was eighteen and had been practicing yoga for a year. As I sat meditating, a thought came to me: "All I can ever know is what I see through the two windows of my eyes." Viewed from this empiricist prison, yoga and spiritual practice seemed void of meaning, and I was ready to abandon meditation and spend the rest of my life without hope of any 'realization' beyond what the five senses could give me. But at that instant I remembered Sakyamuni under his tree and told myself, "Do not move from here — face the void as he did." I concluded the meditation, not enlightened but, at least, convinced that I must continue meditating for the rest of my life.

I cannot doubt that this was the gravest temptation of my entire existence. Neither can I doubt, even as a Catholic monk, that the Buddha is in the eternal Kingdom, alongside his contemporaries Ezekiel and the anonymous Second Isaiah, Israel's exiled prophets in Babylon. I feel a deep love for this man who showed his fellow sentient beings a way that I desire to follow, because I see it leads to Christ: right understanding, right intention, right action, right speech, right livelihood, right effort, right mindfulness, right meditation.

Monday, August 8
Later in the morning, we left for Varanasi and nearby Sarnath, with its Deer Park, where the Buddha preached his first sermon to the five monks who had left him at Gaya, scandalized when he broke his fast and took food from a woman (remember Jesus and the Samaritan woman at Jacob's well).

We took the usual boat ride on the Ganges and visited Varanasi's Golden Temple, but this tourist diversion did not distract us from the real destination of our pilgrimage, Sarnath (from Saranga-nath, 'Lord of animals', like Pashupati-nath), with its temple and museum, and above all the ruins of the great stupa and the monasteries erected by the emperor Ashoka.

I walked slowly through the ruins, imagining sutras chanted here centuries before Christ. I sat a while by a stone that looked to me like a monk's meditation seat. The place made a deep impression on everyone.

Khajuraho, Ajanta, Ellora, Elephanta, August 9 – 17, 1988

Tuesday, August 9

The rest of the journey was given to the fulfillment of tourist karma: seeing the great monuments of medieval Hinduism and the Mughal Empire.

At our first stop, the ancient temple town of Khajuraho, we found scenery different from Varanasi, and a climate less hot and steamy. While still in the Ganges plain, Khajuraho is at a higher altitude, surrounded by distant, green hills. The two dozen temples, already excavated and restored (other temples are still being brought to light), date from the tenth to the thirteenth centuries; Muslim fanatics reduced them to heaps of masonry in the seventeenth century.

The friezes on the temples — Tantric catechisms sculpted in stone — are famous for their explicitly sexual imagery. The fear and rage that these exquisite reliefs provoked, and still provoke, in fanatics of whatever persuasion, is something I can understand. Although I am not inclined to get enraged at any work of art, I can still remember the fear that haunted my attitudes toward sex at the beginning of my life as a monk. Twenty-five years ago, I would not have understood the truth preached by these temples.

Wednesday, August 10

Fear is the passion of ignorance. Meditation on the sacred mystery of sex frees us from this passion. The temples at Khajuraho teach us that the human body (especially the female body) and the sexual union between two humans are at the same time a cosmic reality and a revelation of God. Here, everything is expressed and visible, accepted and celebrated. The images are pure for those who have purified their eyes and their heart.

Khajuraho teaches us about purity; sex and the joy that accompanies its manifold expressions are pure to the extent that they are free of violence, possessiveness, and deceit. The priests and artists who made these temples took for granted both the institution of marriage and the celibate's renunciation of it. The ultimate meaning of sex transcends both. Married or celibate, we all take part in a mysterious, cosmic act of union that is the ultimate end and perfection of the universe. Sex does not exist only or primarily for reproduction of the species; the pleasure that accompanies sex (or by nature ought always to accompany it) is the sign and natural sacrament of its transcendent finality.

This transcendence is always immanent. According to the Tantric wisdom underlying the Khajuraho friezes, every moment of happiness that we experience is an incarnation of eternal happiness beyond the impermanence of both pleasure and pain.

About celibacy and love, I do not need to defend or protect my celibacy. While I do need to love and be loved, I do not feel the need for romantic love, which seems to me culture-bound and in no way essential either to sex or to supernatural love. Eros and romance are two distinct realities. Marriage in India is, for the most part, unromantic. If I were an Indian, my bride would be chosen for me by an aunt or a grandparent. All things considered, I would prefer this to romance.

It is clear that sexual intercourse can be a loving act without romantic sentimentality. The love can be that of friendship or compassion or concern. It can be agape or philia. But love is one; it is not a sentiment. Love is God.

Friday, August 12
Architecturally and conceptually, no building could be more different from the Khajuraho temples than the Taj Mahal, next stage on the tourist leg of our journey. Yet the widowed king, Shah Jahan, built it to mourn his lost love. This most beautiful of all mausoleums, no less than the temples, teaches the same truth: that the love uniting two human persons is God's image in the universe of bodies.

While leaving the Taj Mahal, I met the guest master of the Thai monastery who was our host in Bodhgaya. He was accompanying two fellow monks on pilgrimage to the same places we visited.

Sunday, August 14
The following morning we flew to Aurangabad, our base-camp while touring the cave monasteries of Ajanta and Ellora.

On the wild bus ride through the Maharashtra countryside to Ellora, we saw many Muslim forts and mausoleums. The architectural remains of the Islamic dominion in India are almost exclusively military fortifications and monuments to the dead, including the Taj Mahal. There are a few harems here and there, as at the ghost town of Fatepur Sikri, which Akbar the Great built for his Hindu wives. His favorite, the only one who gave him male heirs, had a palace made according to the model of a Buddhist monastery. The general architectural style mixed Buddhist, Jain, Persian, and even Gothic forms and details. A mosque stood alongside the palace, but within the harem precincts was a Krishna temple.

Akbar's great-grandson Aurangzeb, the son of Shah Jahan (whom he imprisoned), was a fanatic and an ardent destroyer of Hindu temples, Buddhist monasteries, and Christian churches. After these campaigns he built a fortified village near Aurangabad and had himself buried there — "in a very simple tomb," said our guide, who wryly remarked that the British in India are remembered for their factories and trains, as well as for fortresses and tombs.

The Ellora caves are the work of centuries. Starting from natural grottos inhabited by yogis and Buddhist hermits, the carving of this massive basalt hill began some time in the seventh or eighth century and continued until the thirteenth. Buddhist, Jain, and Hindu monks worked side by side with lay artisans, borrowing symbolism and imagery from one another.

The most intensely moving of these caves is the large Buddhist chaitya, with its wonderfully serene image of Sakyamuni

preaching his first sermon. On this side of the caves there are
many monastic cells. On the other side is the great Shiva temple,
with its usual lingam within the inner sanctum. The temple is
patterned on those in the south. In fact, this region belongs to
southern India, and I noted the difference: the people are more
gentle and refined than in the north, and the artwork is more
exuberant. Ellora and Ajanta both came out of the Tantric phase
of Hinduism and Buddhism; they have much in common with
Khajuraho.

In the caves, I felt a deep sense of belonging, glad to be a monk
and to have something in common with the bhikkhus who carved
these cells and images out of the rock.

The next day, we visited the Ajanta caves, which contain the
sole remaining examples of Indian mural paintings. The murals
are of three sorts: narrative (stories of the Buddha's previous
incarnations), portraiture (images of Bodhisattvas and Buddhas),
and decorative (animal and plant designs). They mirror everyday
life in India as lived by peasants and princes from 400 to 900. In
these paintings all life is affirmed, in spite of its impermanence
and the pleasure-pain syndrome afflicting all sentient beings.
Both men and women, at court and in the fields, are naked from
the waist up; princes and princesses adorn their bodies with
necklaces and armlets. Their expressions are serene and open;
their gestures supple and calm. Corporeal existence as a human
being is proclaimed as the best gift of life and the only way to
Nirvana.

Monday, August 15
From Aurangabad, a short flight brought us to Mumbai. We went
straight to the Elephanta caves on an island in the waters
surrounding the city. The boat ride took about forty minutes. The
125 steps from the dock to the open grotto led us to a dozen
shrines sculpted over the course of several centuries. The images
— similar to the Ellora reliefs, with their subtle smiles and supple

limbs — show Shiva as king of the dance, as destroyer of demons, as spouse, and ultimately as Trimurti — the giant, three-faced figure that represents both the three ages of human life and the two sexes.

The Portuguese used these images as targets for rifle practice.

Shantivanam and Assisi, August 17-28, 1988

Wednesday, August 17
My friends left on a flight to Sri Lanka, where they will see the Buddhism not of monuments and ancient texts but of everyday life. Three quarters of the population on that island keep the Theravada Buddhist traditions brought from India at the time of Ashoka, in the third century BCE. I remained in India and spent several days at Shantivanam.

Leaving Mumbai, I arrived in Chennai at 11:30 p.m., went straight to a hotel and to bed. I was up before the wake-up call, having sung the Benedictus in a dream. An early flight took me to Tiruchirapalli (Trichy). Christudas and one of the novices were there to meet me.

I found Dom Bede looking well. After welcoming me to his hut and sharing a cup of tea, he told me he was happily set on not traveling outside India again.

Life here at the ashram is both hard and easy; it is hard to meditate at sundown when the mosquitoes are in feeding frenzy, but at four in the morning, after a night on bare boards cushioned by nothing more than a quilt, it is easy to sit for forty-five minutes or an hour in the lotus posture, under the mosquito netting.

Thursday, August 18
At Mass this morning, Dom Bede preached on the promise of a new heart and a new spirit (Ezekiel, chapter 36): "To pass from the heart of stone to the loving heart open to God's Spirit," Bede said, "we must go beyond religion as outward form."

The responsorial was King David's great prayer for mercy in Psalm 51. After Mass, having meditated on the psalm, I asked Bede to hear my confession. I confessed my attachment to outward forms, my lack of trust in God, in people, in nature, in myself.

"Form is a gift of God," said Bede. "Outward celibacy is a gift of God, not something a monk can be attached to. It is and remains simply a given."

He also spoke to me about letting go of the ego. "That, and not celibacy or religious formalities, is the real issue," he said. "When lovers let go sexually, this is a sacrament of the ego-death."

Friday, August 19
Let me describe the ashram as I see it now, four years after seeing it the first time.

Starting from the outside in, I observe a completed physical plant, with two more outdoor baths under construction. The well-watered grounds are thickly planted; coconut palms provide a cash crop, but ornamental plantings prevail — the whole compound is like a garden. With the surrounding fields and the eucalyptus grove, it is a corner of paradise.

Thanks to good income from Bede's book royalties and the donations of foreign guests, the ashram has no debts and is able to maintain itself, while continuing to finance social projects in nearby villages.

In addition to Dom Bede, there are three other priests in the community: Amaldas (he is presently in northern India, organizing an ashram for women), Christudas, and Augustine, a monk of Kurisumala Ashram resident at Shantivanam since 1984. Three monks are in simple vows: Martin, who is spending a year in Italy, and two Tamilians studying philosophy nearby.

Another junior monk has just left the community; Russil Paul D'Silva, an Anglo-Indian from Chennai and a gifted musician, was the apple of Bede's eye. He used to sit for hours on the porch of his guru's hut, playing the vina and singing. Bede saw him as a son and eventual successor. Shortly after his monastic profession he asked to return to Chennai to complete his training in the classical Carnatic music of South India. Early this year he met Asha, the daughter of a devout Christian family, and brought her to Shantivanam, asking Bede to release him from monastic obligations but also to accept the two of them, as a couple, into a special relationship with the ashram. Bede was emotionally torn by the situation; when he spoke of it briefly with me, his eyes clouded over with suppressed tears.

There have been some instances of sexual activity among guests at the ashram. Bede either denied the facts or tried to cover them over with his compassion. Yet his compassion for human weakness does have a limit, and when this is reached, he becomes intransigent and orders Christudas to get the troublemaker off the property and preferably out of the district. Christudas has no compassion whatever for persons who bring discredit on Bede Griffiths or Shantivanam.

About Dom Bede himself, no question of inappropriate relations with guests has ever arisen. Contrary to what one supposes an English gentleman would demand, Bede has totally renounced his personal privacy. His hut can be approached by anyone at any time; some guests see him several times during their stay, while others, more shy and discreet, may ask to speak with him only once. He is under constant observation by the Indian workers and villagers who come and go in the ashram. At night his door is closed, but usually a worker or even one of the monks sleeps on his porch or on the grounds nearby.

Sunday morning, August 21
Last evening, commenting on the great commandment of love in Matthew 22, Bede said, "Love is not the result of an act of will; it is not within our power. We love by the love God gives us; we love with God's own love."

Love is one; a single act making heart, mind, and strength one. Love, like the Holy One of whom an ancient chant, the Trisagion, sings, is God the Strong, God the Deathless: "Love is stronger than death" (Song of Songs 8:6). Love was crucified for us, poured forth as blood and water on the hard rock of Calvary. Having once for all made love to the world on the cross, Jesus is inseparable from the world. I cannot love Jesus if I do not love the world with the same love. Uniting with his letting-go, the yielding of his flesh for the life of the world, I experience the coming-to-birth of a new humanity from his flesh: Jesus as Mother.

Where is romance in this? There is no romance, only the perfect union of eros and agape.

Bede Griffiths has assimilated the spirit of Hinduism as few westerners ever have. This is apparent in his personality, his life-style, and in the general way he presents his thoughts. Bede's hindutva ('Hindu-ness') lies more in the general form than in the express content of his life and works. He does not articulate a scholarly understanding of Hindu literature, nor does he offer a synthesis of Christianity and Hindu culture. His Christianity is very traditional, in some respects even traditionalistic. He deeply feels his Christian faith and lives it with total fidelity. Bede's consistency with traditional Christianity is not always seen by Christian observers, whether sympathetic or unsympathetic toward him. Hindus see him as a holy man and a sage, one who has 'realized' the highest Reality.

Bede's charism is that of a prophet; he is also a wise man who expresses his wisdom through writing, in which he is constantly engaged. Does he have the gifts that Benedictines recognize in their abbot or in the novice master? You might doubt that he does — Bede is an institution, but he is not one to run an institution.

Sunday afternoon, August 21
There is no hierarchy in love. I do not belong 'more' to God than to what the Bible calls 'flesh', that is, common humanity. If I

belong totally to God, I belong totally to humanity, and the one because of the other.

Being a monk means belonging without having belongings. At customs inspection, I have nothing to declare. I have nothing to keep, not even virginity, because virginity is a quality of the body, and Saint Benedict teaches that a monk cannot even call the body his own (Rule of Benedict, chapter 33). But I am a body, belonging to the world of bodies and to the mystical Body of Christ.

Bede says, "There may be another way, but integration of flesh and spirit is Christ's way for us today."

The hard part of this way is distinguishing between renunciation of sin and the renunciation of something good, especially that bodily union which is the best thing this world of bodies has to offer. Sin is not me; it is not natural but contrary to my nature, whereas the renounced good is part of me and of nature. Yet it is possible to renounce, for a higher good, something that is good for my nature. What is not possible today is the separation of part from whole, of my body from the cosmic Body, or of flesh from Spirit. The Isha Upanishad and the Tantras speak of 'renouncing all things and embracing all things'. Above all, abstinence and renunciation must affirm nature as it is: truly good.

Monday, August 22

Celibacy and hospitality are two pillars of Benedictine monasticism. Bede is first and always a guest-master; his spiritual practice is the adoration of Christ in every human being, female or male, who comes to his hut.

The rule of monastic hospitality is the primary gesture of the monk toward anyone who enters his solitude. Physically or metaphorically the monk washes the pilgrim's feet and joins with the pilgrim first in prayer and then in a meal.

The future of Shantivanam, as Monchanin and Le Saux envisioned it, is to be a 'Benedictine ashram', contemplative and inculturated, providing a meeting place for all. For Indian Catholics it exemplifies the incorporation of the best of Hinduism into the Church, and of the Church into India. It is also a point of reference for westerners, mostly alienated from Judeo-Christian monotheism, on their pilgrimage to 'mystical India', but only as long as Bede lives. Shantivanam is and will remain both Indian and Benedictine. The level of inculturation will be consolidated through the training of the Indian brothers both as monks and as heirs to the spiritual, cultural, and artistic heritage of India.

There will be no successor to Bede Griffiths. He is the last of the European gurus at Shantivanam. The future of the ashram will be the responsibility of Indians, that is, the three priests and the junior monks now present in the ashram, together with Sister Marie-Louise and any Indian women who, I hope, will eventually join her across the road. Shantivanam belongs to them, and I believe they will have the grace and wisdom to live in the lineage of Monchanin, Le Saux, and Griffiths.

Tuesday, August 23
Last evening I talked with Prem Bhai, a Christian sannyasi whom Bede initiated and who works as a lay missionary among the tribes in the Himalayan foothills. He told me the story of a 'miracle' that befell him last May. He was cycling through a jungle between two villages. A local youth and his sister were accompanying him on another bicycle. Halfway down the road a rogue elephant charged at them out of the trees. The two locals jumped off their bike and escaped into the bushes, while Prem Bhai tried to outrun the beast. Pedaling as hard as he could, he continued until he believed himself outside the elephant's territory. He stopped and heard nothing. But no sooner had he put his foot back on the pedal than the elephant was upon him again. Prem Bhai had time only to call on Jesus and Mary and drop to the ground. The beast thrust at him, but the tusks just missed his stomach and bore into the ground. Then the elephant stepped

over the prostrate Prem Bhai, (who shifted his head to avoid one of the hooves) and started trampling the bicycle.

The two locals, observing the scene from a distance, assumed Prem Bhai was dead, seeing him prostrate and motionless between the elephant's legs. But he, having made an act of contrition, felt a great and serene joy, and calmly waited for the elephant to kill him. Meanwhile, they flagged down a rare truck on the jungle road and went to retrieve Prem Bhai's body. At the sound of the truck's horn the elephant moved off into the jungle. Prem Bhai jumped up and climbed into the truck; the driver recovered the wrecked bicycle, and they continued their trip to the next village.

Thursday, August 25
The next day I said goodbye to Dom Bede, and Christudas drove me to the airport.

In Mumbai, I took a room at the Ramada Inn Hotel. I spent the morning finishing the book on Islamic spirituality, which has been my main reading during the time I was at Shantivanam.

I prefer the ashram to the Ramada Inn — why do I have to say this? I prefer the ashram, but I do not prefer the mosquitoes and the Indian movie-music blaring from loudspeakers in the village. I do not prefer the constant and sometimes indiscreet presence of western guests in the ashram (all images of God, of course, but I say this as a blind act of faith, at this particular moment). I do not prefer the romantic, thatched-roof huts, with their spiders and roosting bats, to a clean hotel room. In other words, I do not care about the ashram as outward form, nor as image, nor as something 'relevant' and 'important'. I do not care to decide which is more important and relevant, the Ramada Inn or Bede Griffiths' ashram. I care about monasteries — at this particular moment I would prefer Camaldoli to both the ashram and the Ramada Inn. I do indeed care about Bede's, Abhishiktananda's, and Monchanin's commitment to living in Christ as transparently as possible, within India's great religious culture and the spiritual quest that this culture expresses.

At this particular moment, although I do not prefer it to any other place, the Ramada Inn can serve a purpose and give me a day's retreat, with clean sheets and towels and a TV (which I shall leave off, without imagining that this is asceticism), and a view of the Arabian Sea from my window. I do not mind the Arabian Sea, and I consider it to be just as sacred as the river Kaveri, in view of the ashram, that flows into the Bay of Bengal.

Friday, August 26

I slept soundly in this clean, quiet hotel room, and I was up at four to meditate.

I felt an inarticulate sense of the goodness of God and of life, a concrete awareness that the glory of God is indeed the living human person, as Saint Irenaeus said, even though our life is, as the Buddha said, conditioned by impermanence and incompleteness and pain. There is no less pain in the soul than in the body, but the body is good, in its needs and in their fulfillment, which can be neither complete nor permanent. The goodness of human life and of God is known in the act of accepting life as it is — impermanent, incomplete, painful — and experiencing God as infinite, absolute, and eternal goodness.

While good by nature, could I do better or be better? Of course I could, but my task at this moment is to acknowledge and accept the goodness of God as mediated through, and limited by, the human good. I know God is good, because I know the limited goodness of my own life.

Remember the words of Jesus in Mark's gospel: "No one is good but God alone." Jesus affirms the absolute good with an expression that seems to deny the relative good but does not. If God is the 'only one' who is good, then I can hope to be good, although by a goodness God alone can give me.

Sunday, August 28

The following morning I flew to Rome, and took a train to Assisi. The theme of this year's congress at the Cittadella is 'Death and Dying, the Religious Response'. The afternoon session included an M.D. involved with terminal patients (he declared himself a 'layman', in the Italian sense of 'not a religious person'), a Buddhist nun from Oregon (she declared herself an atheist), and Giannino Piana, a Catholic moral theologian.

Piana said one thing that especially impressed me: "The inability to see death as a part of life is a consequence of the separation of human beings from nature."

My meditation the next morning revolved around the primal act of humility: to accept my embodiment and consequent mortality. Dying is an act, something that each person must do. The accomplishment of this ultimate task of life depends very little on its outward circumstances. Even sudden death may be accompanied by a special gift of lucidity and freedom.

I remember the fears that accompanied my departure for India and every other takeoff and landing on the trip. I suspect that when my time does indeed come, my feelings will be both more intense and very different, and 'fear' may not be the name for them.

Shantivanam, June 23 — July 28, 1989

Friday morning, June 23

Amman, Jordan: today is Friday, the Muslim day of prayer, and I am a transit guest at the Alia Gateway Hotel, half a kilometer from the airport. This evening I catch a flight to Delhi. I am traveling alone to the ashram, but next month a tour group — organized by my friends at the Cittadella of Assisi — will arrive in Chennai, and I shall guide them on pilgrimage to the Hindu temples of Tamil Nadu.

From the hotel room I see flat land, more desolate than

California's Mojave Desert, but oil wells in the distance remind me of home. Quonset huts and chain-link fences separate the hotel compound from the desert, and military personnel are visible. The hotel is a sort of comfortable prison, an elegantly furnished refugee camp for paying refugees. Stepping outside, I find the air warm but not hot; a dry wind makes it feel very much like Southern California.

As I went to my room, I saw two women saying their prayers in a partly screened-off area at the end of the corridor, an improvised mosque for Muslim women guests. Somewhere else in the hotel, their husbands had a nice, big prayer room.

Friday evening, June 23
While waiting for the airport bus, I struck up a conversation with an Indian gentleman I met on the flight from Rome. His name was B. K. Garai; he was returning from a trip to the United States, where his daughter practices medicine (he is also a physician). She just married a man in New Jersey. After the wedding, Dr. Garai and his wife toured Italy. They will stop over in Delhi, where another daughter lives. He was born in West Bengal, near Tagore's Shantiniketan, and now lives in Calcutta.

About Dr. Garai's wife: he did not introduce me to her, nor did they ever exchange words in my presence. She seemed to exist totally in his shadow, as an exclusively private dimension of his existence. In a way, this is a kind of feminine independence from the world of men. But note the independence of his daughter: she studied in the U.S., became a doctor, and married the man of her choice — a lifestyle radically different from her mother's, which, however, is not without its own dignity.

Sunday, June 25
On the flight to Delhi I spent three dollars to rent a headset, and it was well worth it. An audio channel gave me an all-Mozart program without comments, and then I watched the film,

Madame Souzatska, starring Shirley Maclaine, about a Russian piano teacher in America and her star pupil, an Anglo-Indian, played by a teenage concert pianist named Chowdry (brilliant technique, with a somewhat heavy touch). Many good things were said about the study of music and its relation to life.

So the short night passed, and on arriving in Delhi I was met by a man from Swagatam Tours and Travels, who took me to the Imperial Hotel, which was anything but a refugee camp. I sent a telegram to Shantivanam confirming my arrival.

At five the following morning, a young man named Gavin came to accompany me to the airport for the flight to Chennai. On the way he asked me about what 'Padre' means (my Assisi friends made reservations for me under the name 'Mr. Padre Thomas'). I explained that it isn't a name but a title that means I belong to a Catholic monastic order.

More questions: "Does this mean you are also a priest?"

"Yes."

"As a priest, are you permitted to accompany tourists?"

I explained that I accompany them in my capacity as a professor of history of religions.

"Do you preach?"

I answered that I am more a professor than a preacher.

"Do you preach only Christianity?"

I said that, of course, I do preach Christianity, but I also preach openness to the truths in other spiritual traditions.

He then took another tack: "In order to attain spiritual realization, isn't it necessary to isolate oneself?"

This could be necessary for some, I said, especially as a period of training, but the ideal is a harmony between total attention to the spiritual and service to others.

"Have you ever known a person of perfect spiritual attainment?"

I said that "it takes one to know one," and that if I recognized spiritual perfection in another, it would mean that I had attained it in myself; but in everyone it is a process, a journey, and I have certainly known some who were farther along on the journey than I am. Then I suggested that the goal is attained when there is total renunciation of self-importance and of motivations based on desire.

"Is that possible?" he asked. "Isn't the desire for spiritual realization one more form of desire?"

True, I answered, and for this reason spiritual perfection entails renouncing even the attachment to spiritual goods: spiritual knowledge, spiritual power...

"How can you attain what you do not desire?"

The problem is that we do not fully understand the goal; it is not a question of having — having spiritual perfection, having knowledge or power — but of being.

"Then the desire is extinguished only at the end?"

Yes, I said, only at the end.

Monday, June 26

Yesterday, when I arrived at Shantivanam, was twenty-seven years to the day since I entered the hermitage in Big Sur. Dom Bede greeted me warmly and said, "Come; let me show you where you are to stay. We are putting you in a 'posh' hut this time, with an attached bath." The hut was near his and had a view of the river.

I wish I could put into words the happiness I feel. Above all I am happy because, in some way, I belong here, in India and in the ashram. I almost forget the time interval between my presences and absences; in a certain sense I am always here. I dream of India now and then, and I even dreamt of Shantivanam before ever seeing the ashram.

This doesn't mean that all my feelings about India are positive or pleasant. India can sometimes be a royal pain...

We had a community meeting the evening of my arrival. Bede asked me to give the novices some instruction on monastic history every other day, plus Sunday.

Tuesday, June 27

Two young men have just arrived; one of them, from Mumbai, spoke to me at length about his sense of vocation. The other, a Tamilian from a Christian village near Tanjur, has been with the Jesuits but came to the ashram seeking a contemplative experience. He asked me to instruct him in lectio divina (the meditative reading of Scripture, according to monastic tradition). I shall be seeing him twice a week.

We have begun a series of reflections on the Rule of Saint Benedict, in the evening after dinner. Dom Bede is usually present, but he wishes me to do most of the speaking. At the end he adds a few words.

I am overwhelmed by the humility of this man, one of the greatest Benedictines alive, who allows me, a monk very much his junior in years and spirit, to comment on the Rule in his presence, while he listens like a novice. I have never seen such self-effacing virtue in all my life.

Thursday, June 29

After I had been here a few days, Christudas came to my hut and let loose about the gossip that Bede is a 'gay guru'. Christudas was very emotional about the thing; his English was incomprehensible at times.

It seemed the story embroidered on Bede's painful attachment to the young musician from Chennai, Russil, who after a year as a junior monk left the ashram and married. He returned with his bride, and Bede has been letting them stay here as long as they wish.

Christudas attributed the gossip to an American priest, Father Edwin Sackville (not his real name). This man, who claimed to be a member of a Catholic monastery in Slovenia, had been acquiring a reputation as an expert on Burmese Buddhism and Vipassana meditation, and had ambitions to become a guru. I met him at New Camaldoli last year.

At some point, anonymous letters began to arrive at Bede's door, denouncing him for taking sexual liberties with Russil and other young men. Bede simply tore up the letters and did not seek to defend himself in any way. One day, Christudas saw one of these letters on Bede's desk and took it. He found a way of getting a sample of Sackville's handwriting, and seeing that they matched, he went to speak with the American, carrying a concealed tape recorder. The scene turned dramatic, and when Christudas showed him the matching handwriting and revealed that he had taped their conversation, Sackville packed his bags and left, without, however, admitting that he was the source of the gossip.

I do not intend to make any inquiries about this matter. I shall listen attentively to whatever anyone volunteers to tell me, without expressing any judgment, other than my personal observation that I have never known a monk more chaste than Bede Griffiths. He is incapable of making sexual advances toward anyone.

Saturday morning, July 1
The following afternoon I went to Bede and made my confession — sins like being impatient and irascible while traveling, and listening to gossip (I didn't say what gossip). After pronouncing absolution, Bede brought up the homosexuality question. He was totally open, defenseless, and humble. Rather than defend himself directly, he pointed out the fact of Russil's obvious heterosexuality. Bede said, "I recognize that I have been ingenuous; my excessive affection for Russil needed to be purified."

When Bede Griffiths speaks of 'love', there is clarity in his meaning, because of the clarity of his person. More than what he said, it is how he said it that convinced me. Beyond a shadow of a doubt, I can affirm his innocence of both conscious and unconscious sexual passion toward Russil (and anyone else, for that matter). Perhaps we ought to examine the motives and the sexual problems of his accusers and defenders.

Saturday evening, July 1
At sunset, when the sun hits the horizon, there is a sudden red glow that covers the landscape. Shadows disappear. It is now 6:50 p.m., and in a few seconds it will be too dark to sit on the porch and write.

Something fell on the thatched roof, perhaps a coconut. Christudas said that, to be safe during coconut season, you'd have to wear a hard hat around the ashram.

Sunday, July 2
One week since I came, and I still feel the happiness that blessed my arrival. Life here can be experienced as a hard life, but it is also profoundly human. In my case, I feel more annoyance than hardship: annoyance with spiders and mosquitoes, with the heat and strong sun, with rheumatic pains aggravated by sitting cross-legged at prayer and meals. Annoyance with my feeling annoyed. But just below the surface — and often above the surface — there is happiness and gratitude. How fortunate I am to be here and have a place to stay and meditate in India!

Many questions find their resolution through contact with India — questions of faith, of spiritual practice, of interpersonal relationships, of the body, of life.

Monday, July 3
On the feast of the Apostle Thomas, I went with Christudas to Trichy. We called on the bishop, whose name is Thomas. Not having an appointment, we barely got to say hello and wish him a happy feast, as he was leaving for an outlying parish. I made an appointment to see him next week. Then I went looking for sun

lotion, an item totally useless to Indians. There was none even in the two best hotels in town.

Somebody remembered that today is my namesday, because at lunch there was a little bouquet of flowers in front of the mat where I sit.

Wednesday, July 5
After a long summer drought comes the promise of the monsoon. There is now a strong smell of ozone in the air. To the east, the sky is a formidable blue-black, like the skin of Lord Krishna. The crows are heralding the rain with long, loud caws. The clouds groan as with the effort to let go of their burden.

Thursday, July 6
Although the clouds overhead did let loose a few drops, the wind shifted and pushed the heavy rains up toward the hills. Now there is a fresh smell in the air; it must have rained abundantly not far from here.

I took my lunch across the way, at Marie-Louise's place. She wants me over two or three times a week, since, she says, the diet at the men's ashram is totally inadequate for a Westerner who is here to meditate.

She had me eat by myself in the cool pantry behind the kitchen. She looked in on me after I had been served and asked, "Do you feel lonely?"

"Yes," I replied, "I always do when I eat alone."

The meal was delicious: dishes of potatoes with saffron, green beans with chilies, lentils mixed with some sort of leaf greens, also with chilies. In a cup was one hard-boiled egg, and on the side was a dish of rice, of which I took only a couple of spoonfuls, since as far as I'm concerned, potatoes and rice are the same thing. Then there were two cups of curds (Indian yoghurt); I took one, sweetened it with a few drops of honey, and cut up some fruit into it. For dessert there was a cup of tapioca pudding with bits of pistachio nut in it, and I was given vegetable broth to drink.

During the night I woke up with itching forearms, neck, and eyelids (!). It occurred to me that this rash might be an allergic reaction to mangos. In fact, the resin of the tree can provoke a reaction similar to that of poison oak or poison ivy.

That night it rained and at 5:25 a.m., more rain came. The roof in the bath leaks and my roll of toilet paper was soaked, but I still had a supply of dry tissues. While on the toilet I needed an umbrella.

I like the rain. There is a fine, delicate perfume in the air.

Friday, July 7
I saw an Indian M.D. across the way. He couldn't say much about my rash and swollen eyelids, except to suggest topical remedies. Marie-Louise was more helpful; she gave me ayurvedic liver pills and said the edema in the eyelids was a symptom of general strain on the system. My feet were a bit swollen too. Both Marie-Louise and the physician said that I could be allergic to the soaps they wash the bed sheets with. She will provide me with special soap, and have her helpers launder my sheets separately. But I shall still forego the mangos.

Rain in the john again. Not bad, no problem.

Saturday, July 8
India gives me grounding. What India means for me now is no longer high spirituality or what I used to imagine was high spirituality. India shows me people coming down to the river to bathe at sunrise and sunset. If some ritual accompanies the bath, it does not make any substantial difference. Taking a bath at the beginning and end of your day is sacred. It is human to make ritual, but what counts is the human body and the sandy ground and the waters of the river. All this is where God is, where you, O God, "make yourself for us."[15]

If by faith I find in Christ "the fullness of the Godhead,

72

bodily,"[16] then I must follow Christ's divine nature in its downward movement, into the human and earthly. Christ comes down to the river and descends into its waters. With Christ I am grounded in the humanity he shares with us, and there I see the face of God.

What I have just written could be a Christian way of looking at India and India's religions. But another way is to observe — without any theological presuppositions — the intrinsic dynamic of Indian religious history. Everything new in this history has been added to the old without supplanting it, and often has been reabsorbed into the old. There is no 'progress', only continual growth, like that of the banyan tree that branches out, sends down shoots to the ground, and these shoots take root, becoming new trunks to sustain the tree. This means that the Buddha's dharma is really intrinsic to Hinduism. Gautama the Buddha was contemporary with the high season of the Upanishads, and both the Buddha and the Upanishads faced the crisis of Vedic religion in similar ways.

Buddhism never 'separated' from Hinduism, as Christianity did from Judaism. The Buddhist monastic order realized and represented the ascetical and meditative dimensions of Indian religion and stimulated other realizations of this dimension, closer to popular piety. First the Bhagavad-Gita and then Tantrism integrated elements of Buddhist doctrine with the symbolic vocabulary of Hinduism. Finally, Buddhism was reabsorbed into the Hindu soil, like the waters of a monsoon rain. Today, a Hindu who vows renunciation, takes the kavi, and goes off to meditate, in effect, becomes a Buddhist, whatever of Hinduism's popular and ritual mentality the renunciant might retain. In other words, Buddhism in India is now represented by yogis, sannyasis and practitioners of non-violence. Buddhism has no more ceased to exist in India than it has in China and Tibet and Japan, where it has undergone a transformation no less radical than its 'reabsorption' into Hinduism.

Buddhism, wherever it has spread, has tended to 'disappear' into the local culture and to some degree into the local religion. I begin to wonder why something similar has not happened to Christianity. In other words, why has Christianity not been 'absorbed' into Indian or Chinese civilization? The doctrine of the Incarnation would seem to require this: "...he emptied himself..." (Philippians 2)

Sunday, July 9
An Israeli couple has been staying in the ashram these days. I have felt slightly uncomfortable for them, because Bede has been commenting on Second Corinthians, where Paul starkly contrasts old covenant and new, Moses and Christ, law and grace, and also because Bede said a prayer for the "Palestinian refugees" last Sunday.

Night before last, I dreamt that I was trying to explain all this to the Israelis. They said they completely understood and thanked me for my explanation. The dream was probably telling me that they were not troubled by what Bede was saying, and they did not need any explanation from me.

Monday, July 10
Last evening it was raining, and after I turned out the lights, Rani came to my window and asked, "Father, are you in bed?"

"Yes." I hesitated for a moment. "You should go see Dom Bede," I said.

What's wrong with this?

Nothing wrong; I just obeyed the rules and was careful of my monastic vow.

You left a woman out in the rain — is this obedience? How about obeying the rule of hospitality, getting dressed, turning on the light, and letting her in? Maybe it is better to be less careful of your vow.

The following morning I apologized. Rani said she did get to

74

talk to Dom Bede. She smiled, but then she hurried away.

Tuesday, July 11, Feast of Saint Benedict
One wrong reason some monks and ecclesiastics keep their vow of celibacy is in order to protect their reputation and sustain their career momentum. Maybe an ecclesiastic, a diocesan priest, could justify this motivation, but a monastic cannot, because monastic celibacy cannot be isolated from the renunciation of power. The monk has power over nothing, not even his own body. The Rule of Saint Benedict, chapter 33, says this in relation to monastic poverty, but both poverty and celibacy are summed up in the Benedictine vow of 'conversion' (conversatio morum).

Of course, the only chaste reason for being celibate is love. If this is my real motivation, I will stop being afraid of life, of its joys and sorrows, and of death, which is a part of living. Only when I am no longer afraid of the life manifest in my sexual energies, and I no longer feel compelled to engage in a power-struggle with them, will my celibacy be life-giving.

On the other hand, while it is true that fearing life or battling with sexual energies can be a waste of time and can stifle creativity; battles in general, as well as pain and loss, often stimulate creativity. The important thing is to face the battle, pain, or loss with a good heart. At this moment I ask God, as I did at my monastic profession, "that I may live — vivam!" and that I may give life.

Sometimes I feel that my self-restraint and the grip I keep on myself appear outwardly as pent-up violence, which can arouse fear in others. If I could just find the right way to loosen my grip, the apparent violence would vanish.

With regard to my motivations, I am beginning to see how mixed they have been. The primary motivation has been love, but not yet the perfect love that casts out fear. I have often projected on God a censoriousness and a moralism that have nothing to do with the morality of Jesus and the Sermon on the Mount.

Wednesday, July 12

Mid-life crisis and mid-life folly: as I become aware of physical stiffness and aching joints, I am more and more concerned about psychological and spiritual rigidity. At the same time, I become aware of subtlety and complexity, and the dividing line between sin and goodness blurs. I get the idea that the only solution to rigidity is to break away, to use the shock-therapy of an intense relationship, to challenge and question every choice I have made until now. I know the idea is folly, but it is wise to look squarely at it, without needing to act on it.

I found Robert Johnson's *He: Understanding Masculine Psychology* in Bede's library and borrowed it. I met Johnson at an interreligious congress six years ago, but I felt — as with other books that 'everyone' was reading — that I should not read this book until it was my own time to do so. I finished it in two days and enjoyed it.

Johnson, a Jungian psychologist, builds on the Parsifal-Grail myth. Some things in the book I can easily apply to my own life, others are inapplicable. In the penultimate chapter, he makes room in his scheme for a masculine individuation process that does not make me go out and kill the Red Knight in order to get my armor.

Not every boy needs armor, nor does he have to go after the Red Knight. Ordinarily, he enters a Red Knight stage, gains strength, goes out, and wields his sword. But there is another way; a few boys — quiet, introverted souls — go the hermit's way. This is also legitimate, although the boy who takes that path must expect nothing of the Red Knight experience, nor must he ask for the laurel leaves of victory, nor aim at top place and a position in the community. He has to go, disarmed, to a hut in the woods and stay there.

There are advantages in the hermit's way. He is not so torn between opposites. He does not lose the Grail Castle so completely and devastatingly as Parsifal does. One thing, however, both Parsifal and the hermit have in common is the Fisher King wound. For both, the task is to seek healing, and healing begins when they remember the moment before their ways diverged.

Says Johnson, "It is an innocent and often foolish thing in a man that will begin the cure for him. A man must consent to this. He must be humble enough to look to the young, innocent, adolescent, foolish part of himself to find the beginning of the cure for the Fisher King wound."

Thursday, July 13
After lunch, I read a few passages here and there in Yogananda's autobiography, which I found in the empty hut next to mine.

I fell asleep. In my dream I saw many episodes of Yogananda's life, and one in which he cannot have participated: the death of his elder brother Ananta. The young Yogananda, then called Mukunda, was on a cruise to Japan when his brother died. I saw the body of Ananta lying on a bed. I bent over him and touched my forehead to his, my throat to his throat, and my heart-chakra to his breast bone.

This is not the first time I have dreamt of Yogananda, here at the ashram.

I did not immediately write down my dreams of night before last. The fact that I still remember them means that I should do so now.

I am sitting and talking with Pope John Paul II. He is seated at my left, or you could say that I am seated at his right hand. We are talking about something, which I do not remember now. He expresses his own unyielding position. I respectfully express a contrary opinion, which I am sure is no less within the faith than his. He does not answer, but gets up and walks away.

Then I am with a group of politically conservative men — American businessmen, perhaps, or persons who work at the stock exchange. I sustain that capitalism is neither the cause nor the guarantee of democratic freedoms. I cite the example of South Korea, with its free-market capitalism; there is still no "liberty and justice for all" in South Korea.

In both cases, my arguments fall on deaf ears. There is in me a psychic element that does not listen to contrary opinions, that is against liberty and justice for all. I express myself freely with the pope, who in this case does not represent the Self but a sort of Shadow. I am certain that my more liberal opinions stand within the faith, but the pope remains silent.

Conclusion: keep speaking freely and respectfully to your Shadow, in the hope that sooner or later he will learn to listen and make room for contrary ideas.

About Dom Bede's traditionalism and doctrinal orthodoxy: it is the clarity of the tradition he adheres to that grounds his progressive ideas in social questions and his openness to interfaith dialogue. Although Bede personally dislikes the pope, he has a lot in common with him. Bede Griffiths studied theology at his abbey at the same time that Karol Wojtyla, the future pope, was a clandestine candidate for ordination. Their theological culture is similar, if not quite identical: Bede was a Benedictine, young Karol was preparing for the secular priesthood.

Friday, July 14
This morning I went to Trichy to see Bishop Thomas. He talked for an hour about himself, about his interpretation of God's 'cursing the earth' in the book of Genesis, and about the trimurti in Shaiva Siddhanta philosophy. Then he sent me away (no invitation to lunch), asking as he saw me to the door, "What was it you came to see me about?"

I said I had just come to say hello, and then I went and had a nice vegetarian lunch at a local restaurant.

Saturday, July 15
A pleasantly cool, cloudy day: like 'winter' weather in these

tropics.

Squirrels, three of them, chase each other up, down, and around a small tree by my veranda: siblings, or a ménage à trois?

Alongside the hut, tiger lilies are in glorious bloom. A large rose is just fading now, after being in full flower for three days. Other flora: abundant yellow daisies; a potted plant with psychedelic pink and yellow flowers that open at sunup and close in the afternoon; a sensitive plant whose leaves unfold in the morning and curl tight at nightfall or when you touch them.

Sunday, July 16

I worry about my reaction to the old, bent-over Hindu gent who comes to my hut with adoring eyes and joined palms and says "Good morning" at any hour of the day. I look at him and mutter a reply. Today he brought a mango, and I said I had nothing to give him, that I keep no money in my hut (true). Then I said that I was not a guru (true), that there was only one guru here, Dom Bede. Part of me says that what I told him is perfectly right, and another says that this is bad behavior, although I understand why I behave like that to him. I do not want to be drawn into a game whose rules I do not know. But on the other hand, perhaps I am too unbending toward the Hindus' pious lust for sacred figures. Perhaps I should just go ahead and play their game and let them see me as a sacred figure, however ambiguous the game may be. Am I not already ambiguous — a middle-aged Californian who is barely fit to wear the robes of a Catholic monk and who comes to India and dresses up like a Hindu sannyasi? Remember the boy who spat on the ground as he passed you on the way to the river. I too would spit on the ground at the sight of this ambiguous Californian vested in orange robes like an ambiguous Hindu.

Later, Christudas told me that the old man is indeed a moocher, who goes around the guest huts asking to be paid for 'work', even though he receives his meals and a little baksheesh from the ashram. This does not justify any coldness toward him on my part.

Monday, July 17

Yesterday, Dom Bede, Christudas, and I went to a village some fifteen kilometers from here for the inauguration of a Child Development Centre, built by the Belgian Jesuit Father Windey, whom I met in 1984. He is a hyperactive builder of villages, a man of egalitarian ideals who seems incapable of integrating his ideals into the villagers' culture. The kind of education he gives the children, intended as 'liberating', most likely has a secularizing influence on them, inasmuch as it simply ignores the sacredness of the castes and the identification of trades with membership in a specific caste. In effect, his ideology coincides with that of the governing Congress Party. Rajiv Gandhi has said, "India needs a hundred Father Windeys."

Bede got bored with the speeches and the children's dances, and we left in time to get back to the ashram for evening prayer.

Father Windey invited us to visit an ashram he built north of Chennai. He built it without having anyone there to live the ashram life of spiritual practice and meditation. On the way back to Shantivanam, Christudas said enthusiastically that we should send our novices up there for a month or two at a time. That Father Windey does not see what an ashram is for, I can understand, but I am surprised that Christudas is so taken by him. Of course our dear Christudas is hyperactive like the Belgian Jesuit, and perhaps that is why God sent him to Shantivanam. Every contemplative community needs one or two activists, to keep the place running and to challenge the contemplatives' complacency.

Tuesday, July 18

I had a talk with Sister Sarananda, a nun of the monastery of Pradines near Lyon in France, where she was known as Sister

Anne. In 1946, shortly after she joined the monastery, Father Jules Monchanin came to talk to the community about his experiences in Tamil Nadu and his project for a Benedictine ashram. Throughout the years of her monastic training, India was Anne's secret dream. In the Fifties she corresponded with Monchanin and Le Saux (Abhishiktananda), and finally, in 1967, she received permission to come to India. She has spent lengthy periods near Rishikesh in the Himalayas, at an ashram founded by Sister Vandana, a Parsee convert to Christianity. She has also meditated in the cave of Ramana Maharshi, as Abhishiktananda did.

Sarananda is happy to stay with Sister Marie-Louise (with whom she can converse in French), but she objects to Bede's peculiar mixture of Benedictine observance and Hindu-ashram freedom. I try to answer her complaints (some of which had arisen in my own mind) by insisting on the provisional nature of all Christian attempts at inculturation in India. These attempts are questionable, not because incorporating Hindu elements into Christianity is wrong, but because Hinduism is so enormously complex.

Wednesday, July 19
After two overcast days, the sun shines though scattered clouds, and the breeze has returned. I can't imagine better weather. Flies have appeared though.

A sense of physical and psychological euphoria suspends my thought, as I become aware of the voice of the wind and bird cries and distant sounds of humans and their machines.

The wind grows stronger, and mighty gusts drive through the trees. The sound of the wind seems like waves on the seacoast.

Villagers are working in a field next to the ashram. There is a happy, festive tone in their voices.

Thursday, July 20
Rani came to my hut and asked for something to treat a cut on her

foot. I gave her Bialcol, an Italian disinfectant.

I have been remiss in writing down stories people have been telling me. At this moment I feel an almost physical repugnance for writing, because I am sure that my retelling of the stories will lose much of their original truth.

Here is one that Rani told me: Several years ago she was in a village of Andhra Pradesh as a social worker. She was given the use of a small house. Since she was alone, the people advised her to get a roommate, at least for the nights. The owner of the house suggested a local woman, but she turned out to be a prostitute. She would wait until she thought Rani was asleep and then go out to be with the landlord or her other clients. So Rani sent her away. There was a man in his fifties who did work around the house. He was an untouchable — a harijan, as Mahatma Gandhi would have called him. At first, he slept outside on the veranda. But winter came — the village was in the hill country — and he would shiver in the cold.

Rani said, "To hell with convention," and she made him come inside to sleep. The room was long; her bed was at one end and he slept at the other, where Rani kept her cooking utensils.

"He had white hair," Rani told me; "so he was like a teacher, a guru for me before Dom Bede. He taught me about truth. Our villagers never allow a man to remain without a woman, but when his wife died in childbirth, he refused to remarry. 'I buried my heart with her,' he said."

Friday, July 21

Prem Bhai, the roaming sannyasi who works as a missionary in northeastern India, has been coming to me every morning while he is on retreat. Each time I give him a comment on one of the Beatitudes, and he tells me one of his 'miracle' stories.

First miracle: Prem Bhai is with a group of tribal folk. They are setting out at night for another village some distance away. One of them looks back in the direction of the little chapel that the newly-baptized Christians have just built. He sees a great light, like flames, and what looks like smoke. They all run back, some drawing their long knives in anticipation of a fight. But when they reach the chapel and throw open the doors, they see it filled with a brilliant light, which then vanishes. There is no sign of a fire.

Second miracle: A young man, son of the local shaman, has come to believe in Jesus and intends to become a Christian. He is to be baptized at Christmas. His family is strongly opposed to his conversion. His father says, "You will no longer be my son if you let them baptize you." So he leaves and goes with the local Christians to another village. On Christmas Eve he is baptized, and the day following he receives the Holy Eucharist.

On his return home, he tells his family he is now a Christian. His father says, "I warned you. Now I will perform spells around you, and you will become sick and may even die, if you do not renounce Christianity." The evening of January 3, he is sitting by the fire, praying and singing. Suddenly, he makes a loud vomiting noise and spits out something small and white: it is the Host. The youth says, "See. That is the Holy Eucharist I received nine days ago." The family gather around. The Host grows larger, and the image of a man's face appears in it. It is the face of Jesus. They call others to witness the miracle. Then the Host disappears. The young man's entire family are converted to Christianity, including his father the shaman.

Saturday, July 22
Great winds have gone and left us a gentle breeze that moves the leaves now and then, with a soft and consoling sound.

The last three days the gusts were violent, frequently hurricane-force. At evening prayer yesterday Bede asked us to remember the victims of a cyclone that hit Andhra Pradesh. There have also been torrential rains in neighboring districts, but not here.

83

The winds affected me intensely. I was unable to write or do anything creative, or even to smile at anyone, it seemed, except Rani. She left yesterday evening for Bangalore, very happy for her three weeks here.

Sunday, July 23

At sunup, with clear skies, the silver Kaveri shone in its bed. I walked down to the river and saw that the waters have risen since last evening, almost to its level of five years ago, like a vast lake or an arm of the sea, whose waters spill out over the horizon to the southeast.

A general weariness has come upon me, perhaps due to the diet, but also because I am once again aware of how far I am from the real India. The only way to draw near to it is to renounce the attempt to do so in any external fashion, including the wearing of orange robes and the practice of yoga techniques. The only way is to be what and who I am, and to relate to India and Indians on a profoundly human level.

Tuesday, July 25

Swami Radhanath has been here the last three days. He is an American of Jewish roots who is the second-in-command at a big Hare Krishna commune in West Virginia. This community split with the larger Hare Krishna movement — the ISKCON — over the question of how they should relate to other religions. Swami Radhanath's group professes the 'heresy' of ecumenism and dialogue. For this reason, Bede welcomed him to Shantivanam last year and blessed a lamp to be placed before an image of Jesus in their West Virginia temple.

After the American swami had spoken to the other guests yesterday, I had a chat with him. I told him about Camaldoli — he was impressed with my twenty-seven years as a monk — and I gave him the address of our hermitage in Big Sur. He plans to be in California in November, on his way back to India. He spends eight months a year here, on two separate four-month visas.

He spoke to me about his strong feeling of attraction to Mother Mary (the Blessed Virgin).

This morning, I had another talk with Swami Radhanath, and it was, perhaps, useful for him. He professed a desire to learn from me. I perceived that this expression was a conscious act of virtue on his part, and I suppose he says the same to others with whom he dialogues. But virtue it is.

Half the time was spent on the question of why we are not strict vegetarians at Camaldoli in Italy. I was not interested in defending our meat-eating, and I recognized that he had some good arguments against it, like wasting food grains to feed livestock, etc. Then, answering his questions about Mary, I tried to explain the concept of the New Eve, and I suggested that the great mosaic in the Basilica of Saint Mary Major in Rome says more about her than a hundred volumes of theology.

Some of his reverence and respect for Jesus and Mary may come from an inner dialogue with his own Jewish upbringing, which places him naturally between East and West.

Thursday, July 27

The brothers have begun taping the ashram chants and bhajans (devotional songs). Russil loaned us his recording equipment. But first the current went off, and then two of the brothers got into an argument, which quickly blew over. After lunch we continued recording until shortly before evening prayer. I even led one of the songs and felt a bit ridiculous, for the rest I played the tampura. On the tabla, we had a professional musician from Trichy — very competent. Listening to the results, I found the recording quality uneven, mainly the fault of constant variations in voltage. The singing was anything but professional but good enough for spontaneous religious singing.

Afterwards I felt quite happy; I think the others did too.

Friday, July 28

Russil and Asha came to my hut to give me tapes of his music. I told him I would try to get people to listen to the tapes and perhaps invite him to California. I mentioned that my under-graduate major was music and dropped the names of Paul Horn and Stephen Halpern, comparing him favorably to both.

Russil was pleasant and friendly, but also slightly nervous. He is struggling with what to make of me as a person, because he knows me only through my book on yoga. Now all he needs to learn is that before I became the monk Thomas, my first name was Russell (I'm not going to be the one to tell him, though).

Tomorrow I leave for Chennai to meet the tour group from Italy, organized by my friends in Assisi. They should already be in India by now.

Temples of South India, July 29 – August 12, 1989

Saturday, July 29

This morning I left Trichy on the express train to Chennai. The countryside outside Trichy alternated wet paddy and dry paddy, coconut groves, and plantain orchards. There was a fresh, morning scent as soon as we left the station, and after two hours, a slightly cooler breeze that smelt of sea air. The landscape was arid, with nungu palms instead of coconut. After another hour, we passed what I supposed was a manure-processing factory; the stench was overwhelming, and yet people were tranquilly milling about among black, oily ponds and canals for two or three kilometers. Then the sweetness returned, no longer a salty air but a green, fluvial odor. The land was hilly. Great boulders served as billboards; some had advertisements written in Tamil extolling the virtues of this or that product; others promoted Christianity, with phrases in English like "Christ is coming soon," "God loves you," and "Jesus saves." One half hour outside Chennai, the landscape was no longer rural but suburban. I saw a series of temples: one dedicated to Kali, then a Christian cemetery, 'Saint Stephen's English Church', and finally a mosque, as we entered the city limits.

The Christ who is coming to India is the Word that is life and that enlightens every human being who comes into the world. He is present in the land, in the sun and rain and growing things, and in the people when they practice their religion, whether or not he is in their religion. But he is present, I believe, in the sign of the sannyasi, who renounces the religion of home fires and temples, just as he renounces the desire for offspring, riches, and meritorious acts. So the Christ of my faith is present in India. "He gave them power to become children of God ... and the Word became flesh and dwelt among us."[17]

India may be Christian, but my Church is not Indian. I am convinced that Jesus did not come to found one more religion, in competition with Judaism or Hinduism or Buddhism, but to initiate the new humanity. The Church will be Indian and not a religion of foreigners, when it realizes itself as the sacrament and servant of the new creation among the Indian people.

Sunday, July 30

I had already checked into the Hotel Taj Coromandel when the group arrived, just before nine p.m., twenty-three in number, three of them priests. One lady came to the airport in Rome all ready to go, but she had not gotten her Indian visa and had to stay home. The oldest in the group is eighty.

This morning, we toured the city and visited Kapaliswarar Temple, destroyed in the sixteenth century by the Portuguese, rebuilt in the eighteenth, now undergoing repairs. Inside, we contemplated a series of images that recount the penance of Parvati, Shiva's spouse, to whom the temple is dedicated. Once, during her husband's teaching, she was distracted by the opened fan-tail of a peacock and looked away from him. So she herself was transformed into a peacock. But she returned to her original form when she took a flower in her beak and placed it on the lingam in Shiva's temple.

In the afternoon we celebrated Mass in the San Thome Basilica and venerated the Apostle's relics. Last stop was Fort Saint George, a colonial center, first French then British.

This has been a day of grace, a good beginning. Dinner was in the hotel's Chinese restaurant, 'The Golden Dragon', with not very Chinese decor, good but not very Chinese food, and inappropriate music, not loud but slightly distracting.

Monday, July 31
Down the coast we stopped at Kanchipuram, the 'city of a thousand temples', and visited three of them. At Chidambaram Temple, we were admitted to the shrine of Shiva Nataraja, 'Lord of the Dance'; the priest blessed each of us, touching his hand bell to our heads and putting a spot of ashes between our eyebrows. As I got back on the bus, the young driver's assistant (Muslim) smiled on seeing the ashes on my forehead.

On the way to Mahabalipuram, I read the group some passages from Thomas Merton's *Asian Journal*, especially his comments on these monuments, on a broad beach south of Chennai. Mahabalipuram means 'city of the great artist'. It was a sort of experimental atelier for stone masons. Before work began there, about the eighth century, stone was forbidden as a building material in places of worship, since it was used only for funeral monuments and, hence, associated with the dead. The temples at Mahabalipuram exactly reproduce contemporary wooden temples, down to the least detail.

On the side of one massive boulder is a bas-relief frieze alternatively called 'The Descent of the Ganges' or 'Arjuna's Penance'. What interested me was its representation of village life. Men and women dress the same — topless with a long dhoti — only noble women wear a narrow, ornamental band across their breasts. The sexes mingle and exchange glances, relating in a way totally different from later times in India, even to the present day. Again, it seems clear that it was Islam and Christianity that brought prudery and the seclusion of women (purdah) to India.

In the second scene on the frieze, Krishna protects his villagers from the wrath of Indra, manifested as torrential rain. Krishna teaches them to abandon worship of Indra and to come to himself for refuge.

Wednesday, August 2

Before dawn the next morning, I went out to meditate on the beach. Distractions: the temporary loss of my flashlight (I later found it under the sand) and some small, pale crabs scampering about. But meditation is still meditation, even with distractions, as long as the intention to meditate is there.

From the coast, the bus took us inland through the apocalyptic countryside to the foot of Mount Arunachala. At Ramana Maharshi's ashram one of the brahmans welcomed us; he knew a few words of Italian. After a brief tour of the grounds, he recited a series of Bible verses in which he found the same doctrine that Ramana taught: "Be still, and know that I am God"; "I am who am;" "The kingdom of heaven is within you"; "I and my Father are one"; "Before Abraham was, I am." The best definition of God, said Ramana, is that given in Exodus, chapter three: "I am."

We sat silently in Ramana's darshan hall. The intense experience I had here five years ago did not return, but I still felt a sense of closeness to him, and I wished I could stay here.

The next day, returning to the coast on the way to Sri Aurobindo's ashram, the tour members were quiet, full of memories of the brahman's Bible verses and the face of Ramana Maharshi, beaming out of photos on every wall of the ashram.

Aurobindo was Ramana's exact contemporary; both died in 1950. Aurobindo was from Bengal like Yogananda (they were distant cousins). His first language was English; he studied Sanskrit and Bengali after he returned from his university studies in Britain. An unwilling philosopher, he could perhaps be considered a poet who wrote mostly prose. He was certainly a mystic, although of a different kind than Ramana Maharshi.

Aurobindo's ashram at Pondicherry has little in common with either Shantivanam or Ramana's ashram. The main feature is the garden shrine with the tombs of Aurobindo and the French Mère, Mira Richard, his kindred soul and successor. The ashram also runs a school. Outside Pondicherry is Auroville, the 'City of the Future' founded by the Mère. At Auroville all we saw were a couple of partially-constructed buildings — although one of them, the spherical temple, was impressive. The impression it made on me was ambivalent, because of its total rejection of historical reference points, Indian or European. Auroville represents Western utopianism more than Hindu wisdom. The place could have been conceived even without Aurobindo's philosophy.

Friday, August 4
The next day we traveled to Tanjur and checked in at the Parisuta Hotel (owned by Christians, with a picture of Jesus in the lobby). The main event of the day was my fever and diarrhea, a consequence of breakfast in Chidambaram or supper in Pondicherry. But I did visit the temple, preserved in pristine splendor by the Indian government. It dates from the eleventh century, all in pure Chola style; perfectly harmonious, like nothing else we have seen thus far. Note the beauty of the great bull Nandi, Shiva's steed, facing the entrance to the sanctuary as he awaits his master. Around back, some of the original polychrome coloring is still faintly visible on the androgynous figure Harihara. In the southern porch, the divine mother, Sarasvati, sits cross-legged like a scribe. Unfortunately, garish floodlights in the sanctuary violated its hiddenness and stripped the lingam of its mystery.

All these temples are starting to fuse into one. If this is so for me, what must it be for those who are in India for their first and maybe only time? If I never see another Hindu temple, nothing, I feel, will be lost to my dialogue with India. Hindus would understand perfectly, if I told them that my purpose in studying Hinduism is to attain liberation, and that meditation means more to me than reciting the four Vedas.

At Kumbakonam, we saw the Vishnu temple. The sanctuary in the form of a chariot, with Buddhist influences in its decorative themes, has been incorporated into a later structure that partly hides its form.

We visited a Vedic school for brahman boys on the way back to the hotel. I discussed the brahmans' mnemonic teaching method with the group. Italians have a deep distaste for memorization; my listeners questioned the 'backwardness' of the school and the exclusion of science and mathematics from its curriculum. Certainly, the school represents a rigidly conservative culture, and the traditional method is anachronistic. Without defending the conservatism, I insisted on the positive aspects of a four-thousand-year-old tradition and on the fact that a boy would graduate at eighteen with five languages and still be able to make up the rest with one year of regular high school.

In Madurai, another temple town, I had almost completely recovered from the fever. On the way to Madurai's main temple it started raining heavily. We would have had to walk through the muddy street to reach it; so we did not go inside. The following day we made a side trip to Rameshwaram, an island temple near where Sri Lanka almost touches India ('Adam's Bridge' the archipelago is called). Because a celebration was to begin in the evening — one of a series of feasts that honor the marriage of Sita and Rama — the sanctuary was closed for the day. We saw only the outer corridor, which represents a later architectural school (Nayak dynasty, eighteenth century); it has been clumsily restored in recent times. But I enjoyed the savor of the place and the views of fishing villages on the way.

We got back to Madurai in time to visit the temple, also a later construction but of better quality. It utilizes columns and other odds and ends dating from earlier periods. The tour was rushed, but I liked what I saw.

Sunday, August 6

Yesterday morning we arrived at Sangam Hotel in Trichy. I had a headache last evening and today, although it has diminished in intensity since I practiced yoga-nidra. This afternoon we went to the ashram and celebrated the Mass of the Transfiguration. The group will stay for evening prayer and then return to the hotel, except for two men and myself.

In the eight days I have been absent, two of the brothers got into an argument over the recording of the ashram songs, and one of them stopped coming to prayer and meals. After listening to his complaints, I convinced him to return to community life. But the problem between the two of them is deeply rooted, and the stress it puts on Bede worries me. The group will come tomorrow to hear Bede's morning talk, and afterwards I shall see if he wants to discuss the problem with me.

Friday, August 11

Five days have passed since my last diary entry, and I am again at the hotel in Trichy. I did not accompany the group to Sri Lanka. The crisis at the ashram, the strain of the trip, and the constant translating back and forth between English and Italian brought me down with a fever and a blinding headache. The hotel doctor immediately treated me for malaria; however, my temperature never went very high, and I did not experience the chills and sweating I've heard are usual for acute malaria. He administered antibiotics and an antipyretic. The following day, when I started vomiting and couldn't hold down even weak lemonade, he gave me a pill to stop that. In the afternoon he brought me to the nursing home he runs, an absolutely squalid place. They gave me three IV's and many shots and oral medicines. The IV needle was in my arm all night, and I hardly slept.

Results of blood and urine tests showed malaria negative, typhoid negative, no signs of exotic infections. So what was it? My mind has been on overdrive, under pressure on the trip and at the ashram; this, plus the not entirely pleasant impact of some temple images, knocked out my defenses, and my whole body rebelled. It is becoming clear that I came as close to a nervous breakdown as I ever have in my life.

Martin and another brother from the ashram have been taking turns watching over me and bringing me ayurvedic medicines and mineral water. Now I am alone, having just eaten the usual white rice and boiled vegetables, to which for the first time I added some chicken curry. Anorexia is passing. Think no thoughts, lay no plans, enjoy being.

Take these forty minutes until the sci-fi movie starts on the TV in your room, and listen to the sounds of Trichy city. Look out the window over the hotel entrance and see the garden to one side and the chaotic street beyond. Enjoy the cool air in your room; you can't adjust the air-conditioning anyway.

Saturday, August 12
The movie wasn't sci-fi but a comedy entitled *Moving Violations*: a hilarious flick about California drivers that was better for my health than all the antibiotics. This was followed by the James Bond movie, *Octopussy*, whose outrageous stunt scenes I watched with the audio off. This, by the way, is a trick people should use more often: you can enjoy the visuals better; you don't get the foul language, and you are not a prisoner of the plot. This trick is especially useful for low-brow sequels — you get to laugh at inappropriate moments.

So I'm feeling better. But I've got two mental problems to work on: the first is two-track thinking, keeping two trains of thought going at the same time, sometimes in different languages — this can be a useful skill, but keep it up at all hours and it'll burn your circuits. The other problem is my old habit of living in times and places other than where I am now.

I also catch myself talking to myself. I am a compulsive teacher, always instructing this child inside and explaining things to him.

Another month in India, and then I fly to California; at this moment I wish I were there already. I am recoiling not only from exotic India but also from sophisticated Italy: back to roots, to reality, to what is left of my family, to those elementary physical and psychological comforts that console and fortify a person in the face of physical and psychological discomfort or worse. Life is, all told, a battle, but life is good and always worth living.

Shantivanam, August 13—September 6, 1989

Sunday, August 13
I left the hotel and got back to my hut after five. I tried to straighten it up, but I was still wobbly, almost dizzy, at times. Christudas brought me a 'mattress' that he had found, six inches shorter and six inches wider than the bed. I asked Marie-Louise for another, which she provided, and I slept comfortably, awakening before three a.m., after a dream about New Camaldoli. I stayed in bed and tried to listen to the wind in the trees, but my thought machine kept grinding its gears.

Someone was supposed to bring me coffee before six a.m., but nothing came. At eight, Marie-Louise arrived with two ampoules of vitamin B12, and sent a light breakfast at nine. Two of the young women whom she shelters and instructs came to mop the floor.

In spite of my doubts, Christudas did bring Holy Communion directly from the liturgy, and this consoled me. Domine, non sum dignus.

Monday, August 14
Again, I awoke before three a.m., this time having dreamt of
Esalen Institute in Big Sur and of an ecumenical gathering there
in which I am to take part, in spite of the fact that I am recovering
from an illness.

A kitchen worker came with hot coffee at six. No medicine, but
maybe I don't need it. Holy Communion came on schedule. Now
even Bede realizes that I am not made of the same tough fabric
he's made of, and that I have to be coddled slowly into some
semblance of good health.

Reflecting on Shantivanam as a hermitage, I came up against
the inherent ambiguity of the term. Today, 'hermitage' implies
rugged individualism; 'solitude and silence' suggest little more
than privacy. Yet Bede Griffiths, with his doors and windows
wide open from dawn to dusk, bathes in a constant sea of
contemplative union with God, a sea whose waters lap the shores
of every soul that comes to his hut.

Tuesday, August 15
For the past month we have been expecting Amaldas to come
down from his ashram in northern India. He finally sent word
that he will be here next week.

Yesterday Christudas came and talked at length. I suggested
greater caution in accepting European or American guests for
long-term retreats, and he seemed to agree, although the matter
ultimately depends on Bede. Christudas, once again, assured me
that Edwin Sackville was the sole author of the anonymous letters
calling Bede a 'gay guru'.

In the afternoon, Dom Bede came and shared his thoughts on
some of the junior brothers in the community. One of them rebels
against the guru-disciple relationship and insists on more
Christian and Tamil-language content in the community prayer
(that is, less Sanskrit and less readings from the Upanishads and
Bhagavad-Gita). For Bede, this is a sign that he has no vocation

here, since his objections contradict that incorporation of Hindu spirituality for which the ashram was founded. I keep silent on this matter, but I feel the rebellious brother may not be entirely wrong. For one thing, the guru myth must die, in Hinduism as well as here. For another, the Upanishads and Gita are not necessarily preferable to other texts from India's religious heritage, like the Buddhist sutras and the Tamil poets.

Friday, August 18
While sitting here in my hut, healing from my near breakdown, I have been reading fiction. This has helped me to turn off the mental buzz about liturgy, the ashram, New Camaldoli, and other such empty cares. I read two novels by Charles Williams and was bored by their subtle spirituality. I didn't finish the second one, War in Heaven, which tries to be a modern 'Grail' story, but I rather liked the first, Descent into Hell, for its fine, British voice, rich metaphors, and latinate vocabulary. Williams was a member of the circle of literati, the 'Inklings', that gravitated around C. S. Lewis; others were J. R. R. Tolkien and Owen Barfield.

Between the two Williams books, I read Jack Kerouac and felt a twinge of regret for not having read him when I was twenty. I missed out on the nineteen-sixties, struggling with my novice vocation in Big Sur from 1962 to 1967, and then I was in Rome, not entirely out of the world but not totally into it, although meat and wine and Italian movies helped. I did keep my vocation, which at this moment I feel tempted to walk free of, but I am too much in love with the God I see in my monastic brothers to do so.

Kerouac's style is lyrical, metaphorical, vividly evocative of places and landscapes, and effective in creating strong personalities that seem too big for life. The first book I read was *Dharma Bums*, a very tender and gentle story, more Christian than Buddhist. Kerouac was raised Catholic; his surname is French-Canadian, the family being originally from Brittany in France. He was born in Lowell, Massachusetts, the home town of one of my fellow novices at New Camaldoli, who also has a French surname.

Today I just finished *On the Road*: powerful, memorable. All the drinking depressed me, but that's because I am the son of an alcoholic. The travel was fine, much of it to places of my childhood: Los Angeles, Hollywood, and Tucson in late 1947, when I was in the second grade at Camino Real School in the Catalina foothills.

I have found that in my fever and near nervous breakdown, I was talking like a real Arizona boy, with a real Western twang. This rarely comes out when I speak, whether in private or in public. I can't do it if I try; only if I don't care how I'm speaking, but just speak.

Sunday, August 20

This morning I feel happy and rested and clear. I feel ready to start going to the chapel for Holy Communion.

Last evening Bede said goodbye to Russil and Asha, who were leaving for Canada. After supper, in his loneliness, Bede came to see me, to share his thoughts on asceticism and his happy memories of Prinknash.

Here are a few thoughts that came to me as I listened to Bede's reflections on asceticism (most of the ideas are his, a few are mine):

"For India," he says, "the archetype of sex is a divine attribute. On the subtle level, on the level of higher consciousness, the union of male and female is sacred. On the 'gross' level, however, Indian asceticism tends to lump all sexual behavior together, and reduces sexual abstinence to a question of 'preserving the seed.' All 'loss of seed,' except perhaps for procreation, is equally sinful, however it may be caused."

This, note well, is also the opinion of Saint Augustine, on the grounds, obviously, of Neo-Platonic philosophy, not the Upanishads.

Another note: although Buddhist texts clearly distinguish masturbation, which is a venial matter, from any form of genital union with another sentient being — a grave matter meriting expulsion from the monastic sangha — they contain no clear moralization of the question of heterosexual or homosexual relations.

So why does Christianity moralize sex? The question is legitimate but ill-framed. Bede reminds us that "Christianity makes sex a sacrament." As for the institution of marriage, the first Christians simply accepted the customs and ceremonies of the society in which they lived — there was no liturgical 'wedding ceremony' for hundreds of years. On the social level, the spouses may not be considered equal — this question is culture-bound. But on the level of passion and reciprocal giving, the Bible does consider them so. The Song of Songs is not about marriage as an institution (if anything, it is anti-institutional and favors the violation of social proprieties), but about the passion of love and desire between equals.

From the third century on, Christianity recognized monastic life as a valid option alongside marriage. But Christianity is ambiguous when it explains the renunciation of sex in terms of non-biblical philosophies, whether Platonic or Stoic.

Bede brings our attention back to Jesus: his love for children and women, his solemn declaration of women's equal rights in marriage (no divorce for dissatisfied husbands!), his warning against mental adultery, his compassion toward prostitutes, and his total rejection of the concept of ritual impurity. The Gospel goes into no greater detail, and the Benedictine Rule limits itself to recommending that the monks 'love chastity' and 'love each other chastely'.

"We have the Song of Songs and the example of the way Jesus related to women and men," says Dom Bede. "This should be enough."

Tuesday, August 22

Five years ago today, the feast of Mary Queen of Angels, Dom Bede gave me sannyasa initiation and robed me in kavi.

Sannyasa means 'renunciation'. What did I renounce?

I renounced the threefold desire: for offspring, for riches, for worlds.

I renounced home fires and temple fires.

I renounced all that would cause other creatures fear.

The threefold renunciation creates an empty space, a void. With what do I fill this void? With love — non-possessive, non-violent, gratuitous and unconditional. The vocation of the Christian sannyasi is love.

The queenship of Mary, her crowning in heaven, body and soul, are the first fruits of the Incarnation and the Resurrection. With the Resurrection of Jesus, all male privilege ceases. The Incarnation came about in a male body through a female body, but now the divinization of the human begins with the female and extends equally to both.

Wednesday, August 23

Yoga practice should be a process whereby the body discovers strength in its weakness, wholeness in its brokenness, beauty in its imperfection. This is yoga for weak bodies, for those who have renounced all competition, even with themselves. This yoga draws energy from the soul's longing for God. Yoga as God-seeking (Isvara-pranidhana) is a constant yearning for an end that is realized in the beginning, in a "little rule for beginners," as Saint Benedict calls his Rule. Benedict also tells us that perfection is not contained in the rule, just as yoga does not consist in the perfect execution of a technique. Healing comes through yoga when life in the body becomes a total quest for God.

Coming back from my bath, I saw great nimbus and lenticular clouds piling up on the western horizon, and during evening meditation a fine, strong wind came, laden with ozone.

Thursday, August 24

The rain last evening was brief and had almost ceased when we came out of the temple after prayer.

Another thought on yoga practice: the criterion that must guide all practice is the sense of well-being, sukham. When an asana starts to cause pain, stop; when you begin to feel weary, stop. The axiom, "No pain, no gain," is directly contrary to the state and practice of yoga; pain and weariness mark the point of diminishing returns. Your practice may be minimal, but if it truly generates sukham, its effects will be deep and long-lasting.

From Yogananda's autobiography: "I knew an Indian saint half of whose body, in his earlier years, had been covered with sores. His diabetic illness had been so acute that he had found it difficult to sit still at one time for more than fifteen minutes. But his spiritual aspiration had been undeterrable. 'Lord,' he prayed, 'wilt thou come into my broken temple?' With ceaseless command of will, the saint had gradually become able to sit in the lotus posture daily for eighteen hours, engrossed in the ecstatic trance. 'And,' he had told me, 'at the end of three years I found the Infinite Light blazing within me. Rejoicing in its splendor, I forgot the body. Later I saw that it had become whole through the Divine Mercy.'"[18]

Sunday, August 27

Amaldas is finally here, but he will stay for only four or five days. I have the sense that his presence at Shantivanam is a relief for Bede, who is more than ready to let his disciple grow into the role of teacher and monastic superior, so that he may spend more time secluded from both the community and the guests.

Amaldas came to my hut and shared his ideas about the future of the ashram. The fact that I have no official role puts him at ease. Amaldas esteems and respects each member of the community, just as they esteem him. Past tensions between him and Sister Marie-Louise seem to have dissipated. He realizes the need for younger members of the community to experience something of the traditional Benedictine life that formed Bede Griffiths. Obviously, this cannot be had in the open and free structure of an ashram. "The ashram," I said, "is for mature monks, not for the training of future monks," and he agreed.

Looking at him, I saw a certain weariness in his eyes.

Wednesday, August 30
The current is off this morning, and my flashlight batteries are almost dead. But now I see how suddenly it becomes light around 5:35 a.m.

Yesterday morning, Marie-Louise's dog, Raja, was sleeping on my porch, and there was a cat under the rafters, on the ledge between the brick wall and the thatched roof. I spoke to the cat and welcomed him (her); the cat understood and slept peacefully.

Raja comes every day and sleeps around, and in the evening I give him a pancake. Animals love me, even the animals I do not particularly like.

The weather these past few days and nights has been dry, but with the dam open, the riverbed is now full, just as it was in 1984, "a mile wide and a foot deep."

Monday, September 4
Last night it rained gently and steadily, but today I heard great bowling-balls of thunder, much moving of concert-grand pianos in the room upstairs. It rained a bit about 3:30 p.m., and just before the vesper bell, it was pouring. I hope the rain will stop after midnight, as it did last night, so that the toilet can dry out.

I presided at Mass for the last time this year. The Gospel reading (Luke) was about Jesus' sermon in the synagogue at Nazareth.

I say "this year" as an act of trust in God, hoping that I will complete my journeys back to Italy and California, do what work I am called to do, and then — next year, whenever — I will return here for another two or three months or maybe more.

Again, I sensed the veil between my imagination and Jesus. So my imagination is not the way to him. I am to know him by faith, to love him without seeing him.

Tuesday, September 5
Awake at 2:05 a.m., I lay in bed with my fears and the Jesus prayer. I take refuge in Jesus when fear stirs, but the thought of his judgment and the image of him as judge also arouse fear. All this is passion, to be purified like the passions of greed or lust or anger.

I left the ashram with a prayer: "From a sudden and unforeseen death deliver us, O Lord!" But I offered my dying to God, whatever it may be, sudden or slow, unforeseen or foreseen. May I die in Jesus, and may his dying in my death purify and absolve me of any passion or fault, that I may share his resurrection, now and in eternity.

Martin and another young brother came with me to Trichy. A beautiful dawn — small, scattered clouds reflecting the fire just below the eastern horizon — blessed the day for us. We entered the airport the very moment the sun emerged, a fat yogi robed in kavi, ready for his daily practice.

The plane from Chennai was late, because it was carrying the president of India, who happens to be Tamilian and who is to spend five days in the Trichy district.

Wednesday, September 6
I fought boredom in the Chennai airport reading magazines. Newsweek's cover story was on the Voyager II images of Neptune, incredible in their clarity and color. India Today was full of interviews of the protagonists in the Bofors corruption scandal, which involves both the military and Prime Minister Rajiv Gandhi.

My flight to Delhi announced first a three-hour, then a four-hour delay. But five minutes before the takeoff of another flight, they came looking for stranded passengers to fill the plane, and I got on. Swagatam's 'Mr. Harry' Hariharan met me on arrival and took me to the Hotel Imperial, where I slept a few hours. Now at four, I am ready for a shower and departure.

Part III: 1990 – 1993

Camaldoli, June 9, 1990

The first six months of this year, 1990, have been decisive for the future of Shantivanam. Let me summarize recent events, before trying to put into words what can almost not be said, because it is so hard to understand.

In January Bede Griffiths had a stroke. He was alone, meditating one morning, and he felt a great blow to his head; he remained immobile but conscious. When he did not appear for Mass, Marie-Louise and the brothers came to look in on him and found him lying in bed. A nursing sister, observing that his left arm was completely paralyzed, began to massage it gently. At that moment, Bede said later, he had a realization that the Spirit was calling him to merge into the unity of God by 'surrendering to the Mother'. And he cried, "I am being overwhelmed by love!"

Bede realized that the stroke was a grace, an awakening to the mother aspect of God, but also an awakening to his own feminine dimension. This awakening was the culmination of a life-long spiritual process and the beginning of a new phase. He kept the use of his intellect and tongue, and as his limbs slowly regained movement, he and the others at Shantivanam had reason to hope he would live on and continue to bless the ashram and its guests with his teaching. However, practical concerns made it paramount that he not be required to run the ashram in any direct way. In ecclesiastical terms, Shantivanam, the 'Hermitage of the Blessed Trinity' in the Camaldolese Benedictine Congregation, needed a new superior.

Amaldas was the obvious choice. He had been Bede Griffiths' novice at Kurisumala Ashram, the Syrian-rite monastery Dom Bede co-founded in Kerala. Amaldas followed his guru to Shantivanam, made vows, and was ordained to the priesthood. At the end of January, two Camaldolese superiors arrived from Italy and, in accordance with Canon Law, nominated Amaldas as prior of the ashram.

The decision was formally correct but not in keeping with the Indian spirit. As long as an authentic guru is living, he can have no successor. While a disciple may shoulder the burdens of responsibility, the head of an ashram can be no other than the guru. Amaldas himself, while enthusiastically accepting his new duties, was torn between the ashram spirit, which he had begun to transmit to a new community in northern India, and the institutional role to which he had been appointed.

Amaldas has died. He was 42. Thursday evening he had a massive heart attack at his ashram in the state of Madhya Pradesh. He was rushed to the nearest hospital and died Friday morning. Sister Lea, who has been collaborating with Amaldas for several years, sent telegrams to Camaldoli and Shantivanam. Ours arrived during lunch; it said, "Father Amaldas expired." The abbot came and asked me if the verb in English meant what it seemed to mean, and I said yes.

"How can we get further information?" he asked. "Call the bishop," I replied. I tried direct dialing without success; then I called through an operator and waited for almost an hour. Finally, from the Bishop's House in Jabalpur, a certain Father David, rector of the diocesan seminary, told me how Amaldas had died and said that two monks were en route from Shantivanam (probably Christudas, I thought, and Amaldas' nephew George).

Tomorrow is Trinity Sunday, the feast of Saccidananda. What feast will it be at Shantivanam, with the weight of this mysterious death upon their hearts? My first thought is of Bede. His disciple, who was just half his age, has been taken away. With Amaldas were taken his hopes and, in human estimation, the future of Shantivanam. My prayer is that Bede will have faith in the unseen paths of love, to sanctify this apparent tragedy and make it his ultimate witness of holiness, the ultimate lesson to the community and to India.

Rome, December 17, 1990 (Bede Griffiths' 84th Birthday)

A lesson has indeed come from India. Not many days after Amaldas' death, Bede seemed to rise to new life. Some strong but peaceful energy, infused into his body and spirit, made him once again the animating presence in the ashram.[19] The Camaldolese superiors had thought that one of them would need to oversee the situation at Shantivanam; it has become clear that no external oversight is necessary.

I have begun a series of trips about which I am not at all enthusiastic. Last week I was in France for a meeting of the Monastic Interfaith Dialogue commission. This week I leave for India, the following month for California. The brevity of my stay in India — war is threatening in the Persian Gulf — and the proximity of my departures and arrivals make me feel that so much moving about is futile and will be fruitless. But God is the doer; God gives the fruit.

Amman to Delhi and Aurangabad, December 21 – 25, 1990

Friday, December 21
In Amman, Jordan, the predawn cries of the muezzin awaken the day of prayer: God is great! Allahu akbar! But in reality God is more than great; it is our littleness, our limited vision, that make us cry out, "God is great!" When we lower our voice and whisper our prayer, then we must say, "God is all."

I am with a tour organized by the Cittadella of Assisi. Boarding the plane yesterday, I saw a group of anti-war activists in transit to Baghdad. A couple of faces seemed vaguely familiar; have I seen them at Camaldoli? I share their protest against war in the Gulf — this seemingly inevitable war, which, in addition to cutting short my retreat at the ashram, will cut short many lives.

Tuesday, December 25
Merry Christmas.

What does this mean in India? No answer, except the thought that, since that birth in Bethlehem, nothing human is excluded from God. While I am mentally indisposed to imagining the Baby Jesus, I am aware of my own embodied existence with others, and that God the Immanuel is with us.

Of the billion human beings in India, hardly more than twenty million are Christians. But the people of God in this land are without number. God is with them.

At Delhi we visited Mahatma Gandhi's tomb. I talked too much but was deeply moved as always. There is no place in India where you find a more serene, prayerful atmosphere. The rest of the day was spent on the usual tourist route, and then we left for Aurangabad, to contemplate the wonders of Ellora's rock-hewn monasteries and temples and Ajanta's murals. Midnight Mass at Saint Francis de Sales Cathedral in Aurangabad — not a hint of inculturation, but with the percussion instruments and the great energy of the songs, it was indefinably Indian. Most of the liturgy was in English, since many of the Catholics here are from other states, having migrated to Aurangabad to work in local industries. After Mass, one of the priests offered me coffee and a piece of cake his mother had made; he gave me a large piece of it to share with the others, and I put a small slice on everyone's plate at breakfast.

In general, this Christmas in India was singularly good, although without any great emotions. But God, coming in Jesus, in our flesh, joins with us in all we are and do. God joins in our religious life, in so far as it is truly religious, that is, a source of unity not division, peace not conflict, and a cause of our growth in love and wisdom.

Mumbai, Mysur, Cochin, December 26, 1990 – January 2, 1991

Wednesday, December 26
We caught a late morning flight for Mumbai and checked into the Hotel Taj Mahal, the best in the city, across the street from the ocean-side monument called 'India Gate'.

After a late lunch, we went to the house where Mahatma Gandhi once lived. Gandhi's room and the doll-house display that tells his life story moved me deeply. Next stop, the main Jain temple; I was greatly impressed by the ceremonial gestures, all individual. Devotees entered the temple, rang the bell over the door, and moved silently from one shrine to the next, prostrating and doing arati with incense and the butter-lamp before the images of the tirthankaras (teachers, 'bridge builders'). Simple gestures, performed in a reverent and unaffected way.

Friday, December 28
From Mumbai we traveled to Bangalore and Mysur (Mysore), about which I have nothing to write; see the usual tourist guide-books. But I must write something about the finely-wrought temples in Halebid and Belur that we visited en route to Mysur. I am becoming more aware of what temples really mean to Hindus, even though I still feel closer to the other Hinduism, that of yogis and sannyasis.

Halebid is sacred to Shiva, Belur to Vishnu. While both are officiated by brahman priests, they are open to non-Hindus, being owned and administered by the government. Worshipers mingle with the tourists, performing their prostrations and circumambulations with little ado. At Belur, I saw a woman with two young children; her daughter bore flower offerings and her little son prostrated full out as soon as there was a bit of room near the sanctuary.

Sunday, December 30

Last evening we celebrated Mass (with a few Indian rituals) in a hotel room near the botanical gardens of Ootacamund (in Tamil, Udagamandalam, popularly 'Ooty'). The bus broke down on the way from Mysur, but everyone enjoyed the scenery of the Nilgiri foothills and the national forest. In the animal preserve, we saw monkeys, elephants, and spotted deer, but missed the tigers and pythons. There are immense plantations of eucalyptus and banana farms in Ooty, at 1800 meters above the sea. The climate reminded me of San Francisco — the gardens have the same flora you see at Golden Gate Park.

Monday, December 31

Today's journey from Ooty into Kerala took us down through deep, verdant gorges into the coastal plains. On the way, we met two processions. The first was a Syrian Church festival: a silver cross and torches, followed by the men bearing images and arrows under parasols of many colors; then two bands (brass, clarinets, percussion of all sorts) alternating their exotic marches; at the end, the women and the priest in orange cope under a yellow canopy. The second procession: members of a Communist trade union, carrying red flags adorned with the hammer and sickle.

At Cochin, near the place where the Apostle Thomas set foot in India, the boats and nets in the lagoon were probably little different from those he must have seen. The traditional site of the first Christian community, Kottapuram, was too far by boat to fit into our schedule, but visiting the synagogue I felt close to my patron saint. The Jewish community here has dwindled to a few dozen, but from the time of King Solomon until the fall of the Roman Empire, there were continual contacts between the Bible lands and this coast of India.

Tuesday, January 1
Today, the first day of 1991, I thought of many firsts: my first bodily sensations, my first thoughts of God, of Jesus, of love, my first sign of the cross.

Last evening's performance of traditional Keralese dance (kathakali, literally: 'story dancing') was a cultural high point of the trip. We filed up onto the roof-top of the dance school and took our seats, as the two dancers (both male) were applying their makeup. An elderly man explained the face and body paints, made of coconut oil and natural colors, mineral and vegetable. He insisted on the medicinal effects of the makeup, including the eye-shadow (coconut oil soot) applied to the inside of the eyelids.

Hinduism, he said, has many levels of meaning, mythological and philosophical. Mythology is necessary for simple people and for beginners; it is the realm of beauty, symbols, ideas, names, and forms, while philosophy transcends all these. Among the symbols are the many triads, including the trimurti of Brahma, Vishnu, and Shiva; in philosophical terms, these are beginning, existence, and end.

One of the dancers, made up and costumed as a supernatural being, demonstrated some of the gestures, eye movements, and steps that form the strictly codified language of this theater.

The dancers performed two stories: first a divine Prince goes hunting in the forest; second, the Prince is tempted by a demon, disguised as a seductive, young woman, but the Prince sees through her disguise and sends her back to hell.

Wednesday, January 2
I reflect on the mystery of love at the heart of reality; it is on the shared realization of this love that interfaith dialogue is based.

"God is beyond names and beyond all essences." (Saint John Damascene) So is love, although it has, and must have, more than one reference point. Love of God alone is not enough.

On this journey, I have come to know and love India as never before.

Shantivanam and Rome, January 4 – 17, 1991

Friday, January 4
The Indian tour agency did not provide me with train reservations from Cochin to Trichy and from Trichy to Delhi. My dharma, at that point, was to show no anxiety or annoyance. Their agent in Kerala did his best; the Delhi office failed to come through, but after all, this is India.

Yesterday's journey was hard, but did me no harm. There was no berth available in the sleeping car. I had not expected European comfort on the trip, but I did not even enjoy what Indians would consider comfort. Yet the discomfort shared with Indians brought home the realization that in India I feel closer to them than to the Italians I have been touring with. Through the forced closeness of trains, I was able to share the Indian sense of embodiment and groundedness, where barriers are much thinner than among Westerners, and egos loom less large.

I still remember the beauty of the Malabar coastal backwaters, which we toured by boat last Wednesday. The boat captain was a Syrian Christian who kept an image of a bishop named Matthew in his boat and his home, where we stopped briefly. "My church Father" he called him, whom he venerated as a Hindu would venerate his guru or an avatar.

Saturday, January 5
I found Dom Bede a bit thinner, but obviously well for his 84 years. His thinking and speaking were as clear as ever. In his talks he returned again and again to his favorite themes: universal wisdom, going beyond all names and forms, etc.

The others were in good spirits. Martin has grown in self-confidence during the months when the weight of the ashram was entirely on his shoulders.

Christudas told me he enjoyed the trip to North America and liked the Big Sur hermitage very much. He said he wanted to leave India and go live there.

Marie-Louise, serene and positive, has continued to care for the health of Dom Bede and many guests. She is a good counselor for the brothers at Shantivanam. She wants to go to Rome soon, in order to make her Benedictine vows (she is still a Franciscan).

Sunday, January 6

Bede gave me a book entitled *The Church, Conciliarity, and Communion*, written by a Basque Jesuit who was in India for decades but is currently in Rome; his name is Luis Borejo. He argues convincingly that the first Vatican Council was not ecumenical. He says the same of all the general councils held after 1054, when Rome excommunicated Constantinople. Thus, some of the papal dogmas, on which Christian ecumenism is deadlocked, may be re-formable or reversible.

Borejo's arguments are powerful, and they go beyond the question to which he limits them. The problem, as he sees it, is the papal-episcopal structure, based on power, which as such has little to do with divine revelation and sanctifying grace. Correct the power structure, and then, if you say that the bishop of Rome is preserved by the Holy Spirit, not from being deceived but from deceiving the faithful in matters of faith and morality, perhaps you will be believed. Correct the structure, and also explain the historical fact that, for many centuries, the popes taught that slavery was licit and even necessary on account of original sin. It is likewise a fact that the popes before the twentieth century held the doctrine of religious freedom to be a heresy. For them, the second Vatican Council and the popes from John XXIII to John Paul II would be heretical.

I have just noticed the exquisite beauty of the sky: immaculate cumulus clouds set sharply against the blue, beyond the palm fronds.

Monday, January 7
Awakening under the thatched roof after a nap, I contemplated the daylight pushing through it, here and there.

After two nights in a hut on the cloistered side of the ashram, they put me in the hut where Russil and Asha stayed.

I have begun to give talks after supper on the origins of Camaldoli and its monastic congregation within the Benedictine order. Last night, I talked about the perennial necessity of discretion, a healthy sense of one's own and others' limits and weaknesses.

This morning, I meditated on Love made flesh, on the love of the image for the image, and on the affirmative action that is love's imperative. I, a monk, am called to love, and to love affirmatively the divine image incarnate in female humanity. A certain ambiguity in this understanding of my monastic calling seems unavoidable.

Wednesday, January 9
The reading at dinner is *May You Be the Mother of a Hundred Sons*, by Elizabeth Bumiller. She describes the condition of women in India, the profound contradiction of male domination and sexual repression, bride burning, female infanticide, and the elective abortion of female fetuses. In India and China, men outnumber women: for every 1000 males there are 933 females.

This morning, while meditating, a great wave of grief swept over me, and I wept for the dead and the living.

Nowhere in the world outside India is it clearer how the culture of death and the oppression of women flow from the same polluted source. How can the Catholic Church preach the respect and affirmation of life, without a deep, collective repentance for all the anti-women attitudes and practices of men in general and of the male clergy in particular?

Friday, January 11

I have written a short article for the ashram's annual publication, saying that the medieval life of Saint Romuald, father of the Camaldolese, contains a practice of meditation on Scripture that I relate in a general way to yoga. The article is based on one of the talks I gave here.

I hope to return for a longer stay next year. India gives much and demands much of me. I am grateful for the gift and the demand.

Remember the beauty of this year's 'winter'. Splendid sunsets, the sun a great orange disk suspended for an eternal instant over the horizon, before it plunged into the dark waters of the river. The waters of the river turning pale rose at dawn — remember the walk along the river last Wednesday. Remember the guests, their woundedness, and the opening that took place within them while they were here. Remember the elegant young woman with Mediterranean features, whose bearing suggested she might be a dancer; upon arriving at evening prayer, she placed herself as close as possible to the center of the temple, with a mixture of awkwardness and presumption. Remember the young man, an American, who spent most of the day in meditation. Pray for all of this: India, Hindus, Muslims, Christians, the ashram, the brothers and Marie-Louise in a special way, together with all the Indian women who are drawn to a life of sannyasa.

Sunday, January 13

I arrived at Delhi airport to find that my flight was delayed. The plane landed in Amman, Jordan eight hours behind schedule, and I went to the hotel, not for a night but until 2 a.m., when I was awakened and taken to the airport for the flight to Rome by another carrier.

With the Gulf War deadline pending, they held over the flight from Amman to Rome, in order to fill it with passengers leaving the Middle East for various European destinations.

We landed in Rome around 8:30 a.m., and an hour later I was at the Camaldolese monastery. I shared news of the ashram with the brothers, then concelebrated the Mass of the Baptism of the Lord. A layman, a long-time friend of the monks and a member of the Italian parliament, gave a talk at the baptismal font, expressing contrition for his involvement in the war preparations, inasmuch as he takes part in a government that is sending troops to the Gulf.

Thursday, January 17
No bombs as yet. War, waged there and for the motives declared and undeclared, would be sheer folly, in no one's interests.. But both Bush and Saddam Hussein have shown signs of irrational behavior. What have they done this night?

Gorbachev has also been behaving irrationally, in the face of the total collapse of the Soviet Union — the poor man, whose presidential powers would allow him to be a dictator, were he able to be one. He clearly is not; he has failed miserably, and there is something profoundly human and positively impressive in his failure. Boris Yeltsin, on the other hand, has shown signs of great potential ability as a dictator. I do not welcome the prospect of his success.

One important difference between Saddam Hussein and Mikhail Gorbachev is that Saddam still seems to enjoy popular support, while Gorbachev enjoys none, at least in his own country. All dictators have ultimately based their power on the 'masses'; when they lose this base, another dictator usually overthrows them, since rarely do the masses choose democracy. The Soviet people clearly do not support Gorbachev as either dictator or president, but it is still very unclear whether they want Russia to become a democracy.

Shantivanam, June 4 – July 30, 1992

Thursday, June 4
Upon landing in Colombo, Sri Lanka, I took a day room, clean and air-conditioned, had a shower, and rested. No one could say for certain when the flight to India would depart, but I went to check in before noon. I was happy to be there, on the way back to the ashram.

Friday, June 5
By my second evening in the ashram, I felt I had been here a week already. In fact, it seemed as if more than a year's absence was a brief interlude in the life I am really supposed to live, here at Shantivanam. Sister Marie-Louise put me in a hut on her side, where it was much quieter, and there was a foam-rubber mattress on the bed, instead of just a thin quilt. The water wasn't running in the attached bath, but Sister sent two of her students with buckets of well water, enough for the evening and tomorrow morning.

The hut is of brick with a corrugated iron roof — would a thatched roof be cooler? I have a fan, which is a blessing. Out the door I see neat rows of coconut palms, then eucalyptus, then the great and sacred river Kaveri. People from the village walk by, through the trees to the river, where they bathe and wash clothes. But I take my two daily baths with well water, since the river, though relatively unpolluted (there are no big factories upstream), contains bacteria for which I have no antibodies.

The Kaveri is very wide and shallow — two kilometers, more than a mile, from shore to shore. When the dam up in the hills is closed, two or three streams meander through the sandy bed around grassy areas with flowering shrubs like hibiscus, but when the sluices are open, as they are now, the Kaveri is majestic.

Monday, June 8

Misery this morning: a migraine headache. I couldn't find the analgesic pills in my suitcase, and the pain and nausea crescendoed during Mass. But a guest priest, Sebastian Painadath, gave an absolutely splendid sermon.

Dom Bede is not here; he is on a tour that will take him to Australia and Europe. He had asked me to give a course on monastic spirituality for the novices; I began classes this morning. The students were attentive, seemingly interested in what the American sannyasi had to say.

At the evening service we remembered the second death anniversary of Dom Bede's first Indian disciple, Amaldas, together with an Indian Capuchin friar, who died here on Amaldas' first anniversary. A Hindu man, who works in the ashram, improvised a song in the local language; I recognized the name of Jesus, repeated like a refrain. We sang other bhajan-chants at the grave, which was richly adorned with flower garlands, fruits, and colored lights. The grave contains the full remains of Amaldas, since even among Hindus there is no cremation ceremony for sannyasis, those who have renounced both home fires and temple fires.

Friday, June 19

Today is the feast of Saint Romuald. Twenty-five years ago I made solemn vows as a Camaldolese Benedictine. Many things have changed in me and in the Church since then. I still have good reasons for continuing the journey I'm on, but they are different from those I had in mind when I entered the monastery. Perhaps my reasons are better, since they are more grounded in my nature and in the present reality of a Church that is coming to terms with its historically patriarchal structures.

Yesterday, Martin and I went to an impoverished Hindu village to visit Antonisamy, who used to live at the ashram. He teaches in a privately-owned elementary school owned by

Christian lay people without official ties to the Church. They offer education, free of charge, to the village children, supporting themselves by selling local craft work through a charity cooperative in Sweden.

We left Shantivanam shortly after six, stopping at a roadside cafe for breakfast (good food, but the place was filthy). At 9:30 a.m. we were at St. Paul's Elementary School near the village of Andimadam, populated mostly by Hindu untouchables and a few Christian families. The children were gathered in the schoolyard, a broad dirt area defined by four whitewashed brick buildings. This was their morning assembly before classes. The children stood at attention, fanning out, according to age groups, around the flagpole. After the flag was raised, we were introduced to them, greeted with flower garlands, and I gave a short address in English, which a teacher translated into Tamil. Then they sang the Indian national anthem in Tamil-accented Hindi and went to their classrooms.

We joined the teachers for a faculty meeting. A woman read from the Bible in Tamil; they remained a few seconds in silence, and then Antonisamy led them in a song he has written. I had a good talk with the school's Catholic founder and the headmaster (principal), who is a Hindu brahman. He told me he follows a liberation-theology interpretation of Hinduism.

Martin had never seen Chidambaram, the temple of Shiva the Lord of the Dance; so we went and spent most of the afternoon there. We walked barefoot from the entrance tower over hot pavement to the dark temple, whose floor stones were comfortably cool. As we entered, the noon bell rang, and we received a blessing from the fire waved before the image of the Dancer in a side niche. The Hindu men who entered the central shrine were required to remove their shirts (no women or non-Hindus allowed); we observed the fire ritual from a side aisle.

After the ceremony, the friendly young brahman who officiated (frail body and weak eyes behind thick glasses) answered our questions as best he could in English. He has been married for six years now (how old is he? I think he must be in his mid-twenties), but, he said, his priestly duties limit his sex life.

Back at the school in Andimadam, we went to Antonisamy's house — a wattle-and-daub hut with a thatched lean-to where he sleeps and studies. His mother was there and greeted us as sons, with a kiss on both cheeks. The land behind his house is planted with cashew trees, which flourish in the arid climate. The soil is rich, and with irrigation the locals can cultivate rice and coconuts, but Antonisamy has no well. His dwelling and living conditions are somewhere between dignified simplicity and real misery, perhaps nearer the latter. Antonisamy's lifestyle is his choice, although I can see that he gives himself no importance for the choice. His hut is a true hermitage, in spite of the total lack of privacy.

The headmaster showed us a new building at the rear of the property that houses pedal-operated looms. The villagers make bedspreads and tablecloths to sell to their Swedish benefactors. This is the school's main source of income.

Saturday, June 20
I fantasized for a moment about leaving the ashram and its relative comfort, and joining Antonisamy at St. Paul's School. But today I wonder if I can stand any more of India's intensity, the extreme vitality of its people, the day and night sounds of the village, and the vermin — insects in the air and on the ground, spiders great and small, the rat in my hut last night, the four-foot cobra that slithered across my porch one evening, in front of the open door. India is hot and hard and dirty — the sexual innuendo of these adjectives corresponds to a sort of kundalini energy the land gives off. But the sexiness of India is much less impure than Western lusts, the sort of 'sex with a machine' suggested by advertising copy — the female body associated with automobiles and other objects of consumerism. What India arouses in me is a

deep desire for an authentically pure love, the 'egg, not a scorpion' that I ask of God my Abba, and a sincere thankfulness for the celibacy and privacy I succeed in keeping here in India, in spite of the land's energies — or perhaps because of them.

I often criticize the confusion of eremitical solitude with bourgeois privacy, but here I recognize the need to defend my own privacy and to help the ashram's novices learn to be 'private persons', that is, persons capable of being alone and making their own responsible and free choices in big and little things.

Sunday, June 21

Today's Mass is the feast of Corpus Christi, the sacrament of Christ's body and blood. The feast is also about our own embodiment and about the Bible's view of the indivisible unity of body, soul, and spirit in human life. The soul is saved when the body rises to eternal life. Biblical anthropology poses problems for India's philosophies as well as for Western dualistic ideologies. I wonder: is our eating the flesh and drinking the blood of God any more horrific, humanly speaking, than the images of the goddess Kali dancing on corpses?

Thursday morning, June 25

Thirty years ago today, I packed a suitcase and drove up the California coast from Long Beach to Big Sur. It was a splendid drive, beginning before dawn, through Hollywood and along the Pacific Palisades, all the way on Highway One, concluding at New Camaldoli Hermitage around 2:30 p.m. in front of the porter's lodge and gift shop. The brother who was there to meet me was the same young man, now dressed in white robes, whom I had met the year before and who had asked me, impulsively, "Did you come to stay?"

I had written two letters, and the monks were expecting me for a week's retreat. I told them I was ready to stay on for more than a week, even for good, if they would accept me.

Two stories could be told of my first few months at New Camaldoli. A story of joyful discoveries in the faith, in religious life, in my belonging to this earth — solitary and community walks in the chaparral and redwoods surrounding the hermitage, the constantly changing views of the Big Sur coast and the Pacific Ocean... And a story of inner torment, of violent doubts violently resisted with forced acts of faith, a story of sexuality intensified within a weak sexual identity, deep uncertainty about my ability to live as a celibate, and, in the end, an act of abandonment to God and the Mother of Jesus: "I can't keep this vow — you keep it for me!"

While the second story is true, my 'real' story is that of joy in God and in belonging to nature, which has led me to persevere up to now, thirty years later. My personality structure, revealed in the apparently contradictory stories, is what it is, but grace has opened that structure to God's indwelling. The contradiction in the novice monk seems now, in the journeying monk, an inevitable bipolarity, a swinging pendulum in my life as a human, a monk, a follower of Jesus. The still point of the pendulum is meditation, yoga, the prayer of the heart, and psalms chanted in the monastic choir.

Thursday afternoon, June 25
A squirrel just peeked in under the eaves of the roof — seeing me immobile and harmless at the table, she looked around for food and then exited. At the base of the tree outside my door, I saw a bird — apparently an insectivore, a sort of woodpecker — with a red head and a candy-striped crest he raised and lowered, as he remained very still. There were stark, black and white zebra markings on his wings and back.

Recent reading: 1) *A Bridge of Joy*, a biography of Swami Paramananda by Sara Levinsky with a preface by Brother David Steindl-Rast. 2) *The Hermitage Journals of John Howard Griffin*, friend and biographer of Thomas Merton. Both books moved and inspired me.

I felt a greater kinship with Griffin than with Merton, in whose hermitage Griffin stayed while working on the never-finished biography. However, a few lines on page 175 sounded like a description of my own contradictions: "Tom's need to make the total gift of himself to God and his painful inability to make a parallel total commitment of himself to any man, any institution, any country, etc. His struggles to open himself, his sense of unworthiness to be loved at any profound level. He appears to have had such a dread of disillusioning people who got close to him that he acted in a way either to keep them at a distance or else to make sure to destroy any illusions they might hold about him (which was usually a means of putting them off). Yet the capacity was there."

Friday, June 26
This morning I seemed to have gotten over the pain and general stiffness along the spine that I have suffered these last four days. The cause was perhaps a combination of too little walking, too much caffeine, a sudden movement getting out of bed, but also an emotional low, repression of emotion, psychosomatic reaction to a bad review of the book I coauthored with Brother David and Fritjof Capra. Yesterday afternoon and evening I experienced an opening of the second chakra, which I accompanied with prayer of the heart.

Saturday, June 27
An afternoon dream: There is to be a special feast, and I want my Polish grandmother to be present. I speak to her and ask her with great longing that she come to my feast. (I am speaking to her image — is it a photo or an inner visualization?) I tell her I want my grandfather to come too (I 'see' him there, to one side). I say, "Grandfather is always invited," and I am in tears.

The last dream before waking this morning was about

swimming — perhaps in the Kaveri that flows alongside the ashram? Other Americans were present in the dream. After meditation, I walked down to the river, wishing I had the courage really to go swimming there.

Sunday, June 28
Today's readings: Luke chapter nine and the call of the prophet Elisha. He is a prophet of 'the Lord of Armies' ('armies' stands for the Hebrew word Sabaoth, which the Latin liturgy did not translate). 'Armies' cannot be attributed to the God of Jesus or even of Elisha. As Jesus said, the God of Abraham, Isaac, and Jacob is the God of the living, but armies are always about death. "Armies are to break things and hurt people," said General Schwarzkopf, the Gulf war commander. There is no 'pro-life' army. But the other translation — "Lord God of Hosts" — is no better. Wherever there are great numbers, hosts and masses and armies, there is demonic power. The God of Israel and of Jesus is the God of the little flock. The "narrow gate that leads to life" lets everyone in, but one by one, unarmed and with no baggage. We do not march in, on command, shoulder to shoulder; only free persons enter (see Galatians 5). Then, on the other side, we are all together, but not like an army.

Monday, June 29
Yesterday began in great beauty, with a very clear sky and a gentle breeze — perfect beach weather. The last two weeks, the wind was wild and dusty; hurricane gusts brought down some trees.

Reading books found in Dom Bede's library: *The End of Nature* by Bill McKidden; an ecological pessimist, he foresees disasters as a result of global warming and holes in the ozone layer. He may be right, although I am not sure I agree with his thesis that 'nature', as an environment untouched and undamaged by human intervention, no longer exists anywhere on this planet. In the ecology debate, I have yet to hear any reference to the Tuscan countryside, whose original ecosystem of mixed forest and maquis was destroyed by humans and then rebuilt, with a unique attention to esthetic as well as economic values. The result — you can see it in the background of Renaissance paintings and in real life today — is certainly beautiful and productive. What does this chapter of ecological history say about the human-planet relationship?

Another book: *Trance* by Brian Inglis, a well-researched and well-written study of what scientists, during the last couple of centuries, have said about trance states. The 1911 edition of the *Encyclopaedia Britannica* had an article on trance; the current edition has nothing. Inglis concludes with a general reflection on new-paradigm thinking.

Thursday, July 2
Every time I come to India and stay at this ashram, I feel more and more at ease with the climate, food, customs, and whatever else differs from what I am used to, because I accept the differences — the otherness, even the strangeness — of India. It is similar to what I feel about Catholicism, which remains in some ways strange to me — I can't take anything in it for granted. I think that relationships with others should be like this: accept the differences, rejoice in the otherness (especially of the other sex), and wonder at the strangeness you find in friends, even as you draw closer to them.

Saturday, July 4
Heavy rains the last two nights. Last evening we enjoyed the annual plague of flying ants, their mating flight. I also saw two frogs on the path, mating. This morning, as I was making coffee, a big moth dive-bombed me a couple of times, then disappeared — did it hide behind the shutters, or was it eaten by the resident gecko?

Yesterday afternoon, for the feast of Saint Thomas, Brother Martin and I went with the novices to a nearby public park on an island between two branches of the Kaveri. Martin took snapshots of us beside a big, bronze cobra in the rock garden and in the children's playground, where we swung on the swings and climbed atop the jungle-gym.

Friday, July 24

For twenty days I have not written anything, while reading voraciously in search of texts for the anthology that Brother David and I want to do for the German publisher of our book with Fritjof Capra, *Belonging to the Universe*. Among contemporary theologians, Karl Rahner is a great rediscovery for me. I found the many volumes of his *Theological Investigations* in the library, with Bede's faint pencil markings in the margins — so it will be like studying Rahner with Bede as a tutor.

I am also reading Rupert Sheldrake, the biologist whom Bede wanted me to meet in 1984. The book he wrote years ago while on retreat at the ashram, *A New Science of Life*, presents his theories of 'formative causation' and 'morphic resonance', which radically challenge the established paradigms of biology and evolutionary theory, without the least throwback to creationism or what today they call 'intelligent design'. Now I am into his *The Presence of the Past: Morphic Resonance and the Habits of Nature*, a splendid book that discusses the scientific paradigm shift in general and the possible implications of his theory beyond the life sciences, in human learning, in the transmission of myths, rituals, and other traditional lore, and in various forms of creativity.

Sunday, July 26

Martin and I spent the weekend in Bangalore, at Dharmaram College, where one of our novices is studying. The rector of the college showed us their new buildings — simple, solid, in good taste, but palatial by Indian standards. The buildings proclaim:

"The Church is here to stay." Walking about the campus, we met a number of students, some of whom had been on retreat at Shantivanam, all with happy memories of their experience.

After lunch, we went to the studentate of the Oblates missionaries, where we saw Father Samaragon, from Sri Lanka, a liturgist very supportive of our ashram and the ideal of deep inculturation of Christianity in India. Archbishop Marcello Zago visited the missionaries with the general council of their congregation; all were enthusiastic about the Indian rite of Mass celebrated at the studentate, with the exception of the one Indian among them! Everyone spoke with glowing praise of our ashram and of Brother Martin.

Wednesday, July 29

Another excursion with Martin, now to the shrine of Swami Ramalinga Vallalar (1823-1874) — a Tamil saint who preached a monotheistic and mystical devotion to God as Father-Mother and as 'grace-giving Light'. His poetry, in the colloquial language of the peasants, elaborates erotic symbols of the soul's seduction by God or casts her devotion to God as that of a daughter to her Mother. The legend of his life echoes biblical narratives. He was the only son of his father's sixth wife, born after the other wives had died. He suffered derision and many Jeremiah-like tribulations, and in the end he was probably slain by brahmans, because of his total disregard for caste distinctions. But as legend has it, he retired into a locked meditation chamber, and after three days, the chamber was empty; he was no more to be seen.

July 30 — August 22

Dom Bede was still in the United States when I left the ashram to meet an Italian group coming to visit Buddhist shrines in Thailand and Sri Lanka. On the journey, I read them passages from Thomas Merton's *Asian Journal*, narrating his visits to the same places. The high point of the pilgrimage was Polonnaruwa in Sri Lanka, where Merton had a moment of illumination five days before his accidental death near Bangkok. (Next year, the twenty-fifth anniversary of Merton's death, was also to be the year of Bede Griffiths' passing from this life.)

Monday, October 5
On his return from the States, Bede stopped over in Europe. I went to meet him in Austria. He was looking frail, or perhaps I should say, fragile, like an alabaster jar. The perfume in the jar, that is, his mind and spirit, permeated every place he went and every audience he spoke to. It was amazing to see not only his mental lucidity, but also the strength that seemed to flow into his body as he spoke; it was like a reciprocal transfusion of life between him and his hearers.

On September 30, Bede arrived in Rome, and a car sent from Camaldoli met him at the airport and drove him to our urban monastery of San Gregorio. We showed him to his room, but he said, "No, I do not wish to stay in Rome. The car is here; please take me straightaway to Camaldoli." It was a day of heavy rain, which grew heavier as the car advanced north on the Autostrada del Sole. Half way to the monastery, the car broke down. The driver called Camaldoli, and they sent another car. Bede waited patiently and chatted cheerfully until the other vehicle came.

Bede arrived at the Monastery of Camaldoli in mid-afternoon, just as the sun broke through the clouds. The abbot, Dom Emanuele, who was in bed with a fever, put on his robes and came down to greet Dom Bede. We have a photograph of the two of them, standing in a doorway leading to the cloister garden, surrounded by a halo of pale sunlight. Another photo shows Bede seated alone in the monastic choir, wearing the wide-sleeved robe of the Camaldolese. He told us of his joy in being clothed once again as a 'white monk', like those at his original monastery in England. The following day two novices pronounced their vows, and Bede gave them his blessing as they were clothed with the cowl. He was radiant, and so were they.

While at the monastery, Bede asked me to accompany him the following year on a trip to South Africa. I had private doubts about the possibility of his traveling again, but I said yes. On Bede's return to Shantivanam, the brothers later told me, he was continually speaking about the Camaldolese. His last visit to Camaldoli was a 'return to the center' of his monastic vocation.

Letter to South African friend of Dom Bede, January 28, 1993

Dear Br. John,

Thank you for your letter of 9 January, with the copy of your letter to Dom Bede. It appears that, unfortunately, you have not been informed of the grave state of Father's health.

I received your program for his tour of South Africa in December and was about to write you, when we got word that he had had a stroke and was in coma at the Catholic hospital in Trichy. This was right before Christmas. Then early this month, Father regained consciousness and use of speech, but remained paralyzed on his left side. He was able to come to chapel for evening prayer in a wheel chair. In mid-January, our Father Bernardino Cozzarini, a Camaldolese monk and longtime friend of Dom Bede, arrived at Shantivanam, along with the former prior of New Camaldoli, who plans to stay for a few months. At that time, it was uncertain whether there was any hope for improvement.

Last Monday, a call came from Father Bernardino, now joined by another Camaldolese superior, that Dom Bede's health has taken a turn for the worse. It seems that the hour is close at hand, when he will close his eyes on this world. In the event of his demise, we shall be informed immediately by our brothers at the ashram, and I shall relay the news to you by telephone.

It does not seem reasonable to hope for a miraculous cure at this point. Surely, only a miracle would suffice for Bede to fulfill his and your plans for South Africa. For my part, I would have been very honored to accompany him and to visit your country. If God wills, perhaps there will be another occasion.

As it is, I suggest you communicate the news of Father's illness to those who were planning to welcome him, and ask their prayers. God's will be done in him, in us, and in all.

Camaldoli and Rome, May 13-15, 1993

Thursday, May 13
I telephoned India again, just after four a.m. (just before eight their time), and Christudas said Bede would probably not live to see another day. So I can't go to California now. This morning I get my certificate of residence in the nearby township; in the afternoon I go to Rome with Dom Emanuele; tomorrow I apply for my Indian visa, purchase tickets and travelers' cheques, and I am ready to leave.

Christudas called Camaldoli again during lunch. Bede passed away at 4:30 p.m. Indian time, one p.m. in Italy.

Saturday, May 15
All things work together for the good, said Saint Paul. I imagine that Dom Bede, the transcendent 'perfect English gentleman', was so kind as to wait until the Italian psalm book (most of whose music I wrote) was printed and I had seen it, before he required my presence at Shantivanam. Even the trip has been arranged with special kindness, and my flight to Colombo makes convenient connections with Sunday's flight to Trichy, where I am due to arrive at 2:15 p.m.

Today, Bede Griffiths was laid to rest alongside the temple at Shantivanam.

The signs of God's good favor on my traveling reassure me that my stay in India will be for the good of all, and that I shall have the strength to deal with the many problems that will arise on the death of Dom Bede. But 'to have the strength' means to have it, not of myself, but solely from God. I am weak, and I am willing to appear to be what I am, so that God's strength, which appears weak in human eyes, may be what it is.

This is a time for meditation. Do not do anything! Do not go anywhere! The spirit of the three founders of the ashram is moving, and we can keep pace with them only by sitting still; if we try to move, they will outstrip us.

Of the three 'hermits of Saccidananda', Monchanin taught us sat (being as co-esse); Le Saux taught us cit (consciousness); Griffiths taught us ananda (joy).

Dom Bede had no more need to meditate than a stone has need to meditate. The inside and the outside of a stone are all stone, one and the same. Bede had cracked his ego wide open; he had shattered the shell of illusion; he had let the Spirit in. So inside and outside were one, all meditation.

Shantivanam, May 16 – August 2, 1993

Sunday, May 16
I arrived in Colombo around six a.m. At noon, I left on the flight to Trichy. Christudas and his sister, a nurse at the local Catholic hospital, met me at the airport, where the mostly useless security measures had been tightened after a Tamilian killed Sri Lanka's president.

At the ashram, I changed into kavi and celebrated Mass for Bede's soul, and did arati (flame offering) at his grave.

Monday morning, May 17
The weather here was not as hot as I expected it to be.

Slowly and painfully, the brothers began to recount the circumstances of Bede's passing. He was speaking and asking questions up to the very end. His mental confusion consisted mostly in the loss of a sense of time and the sequence of events. He recited traditional prayers and prayed in his own words. There was no agony or death rattle. His last breaths were soft, barely sighs, and their cessation was imperceptible.

His body remained dry and his skin fresh more than forty-eight hours after death, until he was buried. He was not embalmed.

Monday evening, May 17
I found Marie-Louise in a state of profound grief. But today she was more at ease, and she shared with me some events of Dom Bede's last week.

Early in the morning on Saturday, May 9, he told her, "I must go to the Camaldolese. They are waiting for me." She tried to explain that Camaldoli was very far away, in Italy, but he kept insisting. "I must go to the Camaldolese!"

Bede, said Marie-Louise, was an evening person. He was most full of energy at the time of Vespers.

Christudas told me that Bede, in the weeks following his return from Europe and the visit to Camaldoli, repeatedly expressed his admiration for the Camaldolese, his sense of the bonding with them as a great, good fortune, and his esteem for the abbot, who, he said, got up from his sick bed to welcome him.

Tuesday, May 18
Last night it was mild and clear, but at an hour close to midnight a heavy thundershower began abruptly, accompanied by strong winds. I awoke to the storm sounds, listened a few minutes, and drifted back into sleep.

This morning I presided at Mass. Jesus said, "If I do not go, the Paraclete will not come to you." No one could ask Bede, "Where are you going?" There are neither "where" nor "when" in God, who was Bede's destination.

After Mass a guest told me the following:

She and a few others were meditating in front of Bede's hut. They had set up a small table on the porch under the thatched-roof overhang, with a framed photograph of him and a small oil lamp. When the prayer bell rang at nine, they left everything as it was (the air was perfectly calm) and went to the temple. Then they retired for the night. When she got up at four this morning and saw that the storm had torn branches off trees and scattered clothes hung out to dry, she ran to Bede's hut, to see what had become of the photograph. She found the tabletop dry, and the photo, which had been leaning against the wall, had not budged an inch, nor had the oil lamp.

Wednesday, May 19
As Marie-Louise was putting a white cloth on Bede's chest, to protect his one remaining lung, he asked her to cover his legs also: "Because of my anointing," he said.

I feel so much at home here, that I lose the sense of passing time. Less than sixty hours after arriving at the ashram, it seems I have been here months, or rather, that my absence has been insignificant.

Siegfried Stricker (not his real name), who came to the funeral and then departed abruptly when he saw me arrive, was claiming that Dom Bede and Christudas had authorized him to speak in Bede's name at the Parliament of Religions in Chicago this August. He also sent a forty-one page article to the Tablet. But they had already received and published our press release.

Thursday, May 20
Other gems from Dom Bede's last days:
They took him to an Ayurvedic hospital in Kerala last February. As they were speaking about ayurvedic this and ayurvedic that, he understood them to say that he was to take part in Vedic rituals, and he said, "I cannot; that is not my tradition."
Toward the end, in addition to the Lord's Prayer and the Hail

Mary, Bede repeated very slowly, again and again, the Jesus prayer: "Lord Jesus Christ, Son of God, have mercy on me a sinner." He would often insert a pause before the words, "a sinner." He said that this prayer expressed the entire meaning of his faith and had become so much a part of him that it repeated itself as if it were of its own will. "But of course," he said to Marie-Louise, "this is not really my tradition, as it is yours, since you are Orthodox." Apparently Bede, at that moment, mistook Marie-Louise for another person, a Syrian Orthodox woman.

Marie Louise said that Bede never loved her but always blessed her. When the Camaldolese Mother Abbess was here from Rome, they asked him if he was glad that Marie-Louise was to make her profession as a Camaldolese and to affiliate her ashram with the monastery in Italy. Bede replied, "I give Marie-Louise and Ananda Ashram my blessing."

Bede Griffiths' insistence on the integrity of 'my tradition' — that is, Catholic Christianity — was nothing new, nor was it the consequence of some sort of senile regression brought on by the stroke. On one occasion, years ago, he heard a group of European guests at Shantivanam singing "Hare Krishna, Hare Ram" in the temple. Immediately, he went in and told them, politely but sternly, that this was a Christian temple, and Hindu worship was not allowed in it.

Friday, May 21
Yesterday afternoon I meditated in Bede's hut, remembering his dying at that hour, one week ago. If ever a death could be called beautiful, his was, and yet death is always ugly. It is right, in the words of Dylan Thomas, to "rage, rage against the dying of the light."

Rani was here when I arrived. She told me that last November — when Bede was in reasonably good health — she dreamt she saw him lying dead on a bier. Then the living Bede appeared standing and said to her, "You will see me once more before I go."

She arranged to come for a retreat in mid-May, and although she had heard, early in the year, that her guru was seriously ill, she received no word of his death. She arrived on May 15, just before the funeral. She saw him laid out in the temple, before he was placed in the coffin and buried.

Many others dreamed of him during his illness. The other day an Italian guest arrived and came to my hut. He told me his dream: "I did not know Dom Bede was ill. In my dream I saw him lying on the cot in his cell, surrounded by the Indian brothers and sisters. But he seemed strange, because he was not wearing his usual orange robe but was covered in white." I told him that Marie-Louise had placed a white cloth over him shortly before his passing.

Saturday, May 22

In this morning's gospel reading, John 16:23-28, Jesus says, "On that day you will ask me nothing." Two senses of the verb, 'to ask': asking questions and making requests. I have no more questions, at least none about "the way, the truth, and the life". Now I am able to say, "My Lord and my God," beyond grammar and syntax, beyond the distinction between declarative and interrogative sentences. Requests can now be made directly to the Father, because the mediation of the name of Jesus transcends mediation itself: "Whoever sees me, sees the Father."

Monday, May 24

Christudas had a tape recorder running while he was caring for Bede. Martin also made recordings of their guru during nights spent at his bedside. As an 'evening person', Bede had some of his best thoughts during the late hours, and with someone there to express them to, he would talk on and on. Most of these conversations revolved around his physical condition; often they betrayed the state of confusion that resulted from his loss of space-time reference points. He retained his sanity; concepts remained clear, and his train of thought was, for the most part, logical. Yet there were moments when, as Mariè-Louise put it, his spirit rose above the weakened body and brain, and Bede became the very voice of wisdom and love. His speech patterns became less self-consciously 'Oxfordian'; some of the British gentleman fell away, and he let himself demonstrate affection, tenderness, and childlike joy, such as never before had they seen in him.

During his months of agony, Bede had to struggle to frame his relationships with persons in time and space. He was often unsure where people were and how long they had been there. At one point he saw Martin as Amaldas and criticized him for being away from Shantivanam so long. Later, speaking of Amaldas in the third person, Bede said, "He and I have little in common, because our personalities are so different." This is the sort of expression Bede used when referring to persons with whom he was in disagreement or whom he did not like.

I listened to these tapes, rewinding and repeating passages until the muttered words, disturbed by extraneous noises, came clear.

On April 26, responding to Martin's request — "You have to impart your grace to me" — Bede said, "I really want you and Christudas and Amaldas and me to be living together as brothers in unity — that is what 'grace' is in my life," quoting the Latin antiphon he had sung so often at Vespers: Ecce quam bonum et quam iucundum habitare fratres in unum — "Behold how good and how pleasant it is, living as brothers in unity." Dom Bede had only this grace to impart.

Each brother was to have his unique role in the community. To Martin, Bede said: "You have a very clear, decisive character... I see in you a leader who will organize and bring together a community in an effective way. That is a unique gift; you have a gift to do this. That is what I really recognize in you. I am thinking about Christudas. How do you see Christudas?"

Martin answered, "Christudas is a very good administrator."

"Do you recognize Christudas as the administrator of our community?" asked Bede.

"Yes," replied Martin.

Bede continued: "We have relations of friendship with very many other groups. Dom Bede is the head of the community. And Brother Martin has a very singular contribution to make. Could we make a framework for Shantivanam along those lines?" Martin answered in the affirmative, and Bede told him to put it down in writing.

Martin asked about me: "Will Father Thomas be part of the community?"

"Yes," said Bede.

"As superior?"

"Yes."

Wednesday, May 26

Dom Bede received the anointing of the sick on Wednesday, May 12. He had been in and out of coma during the preceding five days, but upon receiving the sacrament he regained consciousness. During the night, most of the community was with him, and Christudas set up his cassette recorder behind Bede's pillow.

Listening to the tape, I heard him struggling to say something. Mixed with other voices and various sounds, the name 'Benedict' came through, and I rewound the tape.

"Help… will you help me?" asked Bede.

Christudas responded clearly, "We are here to help you, my dear."

Then Bede, struggling to raise his voice, gasped a phrase that ended in "choich." This did not seem to be 'choice'; so I supposed he was saying 'church' in his non-Oxfordian, childhood accent. Increasing the volume and rewinding the tape, I listened again to the phrase until it was clear to me that he was saying:

"Let me die in the church, just as Saint Benedict."

I remembered Saint Gregory the Great's account of Saint Benedict's dying, when he asked his monks to carry him into the oratory and to hold him up on his feet as he received viaticum, the last Holy Communion.

The feeble voice continued: "They hold him in his place in choir..." Bede corrected his use of the present tense, "They held him in choir, in choir... help me." This was Bede Griffiths' last wish.

Thursday, May 27
While I was listening to the tapes, a young man from Mangalore, Maxim, came to my hut. Born in 1965, he was seriously injured at age ten and remained slightly handicapped in his extremities and in his speech (not very noticeable). He was praying to Jesus that he might find 'a selfless path', and he was attracted to the ashram.

What sense or purpose does a spiritual life have, other than to be like God, bonum diffusivum sui, "the Good that spreads itself abroad"? This is not a goodness I can ascribe to myself, or others to me, but the goodness that makes people be good and 'feel' (know themselves as) good.

The two sayings, "If it feels good, do it," and "Rules are made to be broken," like Saint Augustine's maxim, "Love, and do what you will," are as dangerous as fire, but they are also as useful as fire. Being good is also a 'feeling' — an awareness of one's present state as good and as related to goodness as such. You cannot do good or be good unless you 'feel good', that is, unless you experience here and now the goodness of your being, of the direction you are moving, of the action you are performing.

A clear concept of the good — even a 'higher' good or the 'common' good — is not enough. I can choose a higher or common good or a long-term good only when I have in some way experienced the connaturality of my being and my present state with that good, or in other words, when I feel it is good for me, inasmuch as I am part of a higher and greater Me. 'Rules' exist to give form ('art') to the creative impulse, but it is of the nature of the creative impulse to make new rules, which, being new, break the old. There is no art without rules, and there is no good art without new rules that break the old ones and make the work itself new. Finally, loving is 'doing what you will'. The expression, 'free love', extended beyond a narrowly sexual connotation, is a tautology. We love to the extent that we are free. My love is true to the extent that it makes me and the one I love free. Perhaps we should talk about 'freeing love', love that makes us free, because it is also truth.

Friday, May 28
I complained to Christudas about my aches and pains, the result of the usual rheumatism combined with jet lag, and he ordered one of the workers to give me an oil massage every afternoon for the next couple of weeks. Yesterday, the man came as usual around five p.m., but I sent him away, since we had been all day without electricity and running water, and I would have had no way of washing off the heavy ayurvedic oils. However, by six we had water again, and the electric light was on most of the evening, with few interruptions.

Saturday, May 29
Today is the last weekday of Easter time: the Gospel (John 21) gives us the "other disciple," the "one who remains," while Peter is led away bound. The other disciple, the one whom Jesus loves, is a figure of contemplative witness, charismatic and not institutional, or perhaps he represents the sages of India, before and after Jesus — Yajñavalkya, Buddha, Ramana Maharshi, Anandamoyi Ma...

Sunday, May 30
Pentecost: after the fiery pains shooting up my left thigh, which — thanks to the oil massage — are close to vanishing, now I have a

terrific cramp in my lower back. I alleviated it somewhat by doing yoga movements. I keep coming back to the idea of these pains being the consequence of some sort of kundalini phenomenon.

Tuesday, June 1

Yesterday I had some thoughts about Dom Bede's Benedictine formation in relation to his Indian experience, but I did not write them down. They had something to do with cosmic revelation and the Cosmic Christ, and being grounded (monastic stability) in the cosmic rhythms of monastic prayer (the Divine Office). For Marie-Louise, Bede's monastic qualities during his last days were honesty, humility, and his faithfulness to the bell, the times of prayer, and the 'groundedness' of meditation.

I have sent a fax to Barbara Bernstein, one of the organizers of the Chicago Parliament of Religions, asking her to invite Brother Martin to present a testimonial to Bede Griffiths. Bede himself had long ago been invited to be one of the principal speakers, and they plan to have a special commemoration ceremony for him during the event.

Friday, June 4

A plague of gnats came last evening. After supper, the porch and the door of my hut were plastered with them, attracted by the light over the entrance. As I crushed them under my sandals, they gave off a resinous odor. They were also going for the massage oil.

Rain in the night again. Humid and relatively cool today.

Arulraj, a sixteen-year-old villager (short and frail — I thought he was about thirteen) works in the kitchen and brings me the thermos with boiled water. He comes often to the temple, wearing an orange tee-shirt with an image of Saint Benedict printed on it. He speaks a few words of English. On seeing the gnats, he said, "Hang pepper with coconut oil" — some kind of remedy or repellent.

Saturday, June 5

Gratitude for life, even in its brokenness. Gratitude for my monastic life, even though imperfect. It is good to know that I am imperfect; it is good to be poor and needy. I can be grateful for even a minimal share in the 'life of the world', the great common good of humanity. I give my 'widow's mites'.

The floating pericope of John 7, 53-8, 11 (about who may 'cast the first stone') is absent from some ancient manuscripts. The words of Jesus to the adulteress, "Neither do I condemn you," create enormous difficulties, not only for moralists but also for those who say, 'Jesus was God; he knew everything; he could never sin; he never defiled himself with women,' etc. Either God is unacceptably permissive, or else Jesus counts himself among those not empowered to stone her, because they are not without sin. Of course, "Neither do I condemn you," does not necessarily imply, 'I'm a sinner like the rest', but it does mean what it says.

The text says nothing and implies nothing about the woman's supposed repentance. If Jesus does not condemn her, it is not because she is penitent, but simply because she is accused and is, in fact, guilty. As he said of the sinful woman in Luke, who had washed his feet with her tears, Jesus would have said to the adulteress, "Much is forgiven you, because you have loved much," not: "Much is forgiven you, because you are so abjectly repentant."

Monday, June 7

These days, the mealtime reading has been Beatrice Bruteau's *Radical Optimism: Rooting Ourselves in Reality* (New York: Crossroad, 1993). A lovely book, but I am taken aback by what she writes on pages 31-32: "A life of regular habits and the deepened authenticity released by silence reduce the problem of disordered desires considerably. The desires of the senses are more teachable and changeable, I think, than we often give them credit for being. New tastes can be acquired and old ones forsaken sometimes in a matter of days, and by almost everyone in a matter of weeks, if there is the will to have it so."

She speaks of 'hardening of the heart' and offers a three-step method for softening it: Understanding-Determination-Practice. But what about the irremediably broken, Humpty-Dumpty hearts, which all the understanding and determination and practice in the world can never put back together again?

I think that God draws many people into contemplative prayer through their experience of brokenness, weakness, and lack of will-power. This has been my experience and still is my path, even after thirty years as a contemplative monk.

Otherwise, the book is splendid.

Thursday, June 10
Lots of wind, beautiful clouds, occasional evening and night rains, while Kerala across the mountains is being drenched in its monsoon.

Prem Bhai, the lay missionary, arrived Monday, and we have had a couple of good talks. He told me his latest stories:

1. A border cop arrested him as he was leaving the Himalayan foothills for Assam, but the officer really wanted him to come to his home and baptize him, together with his whole family.

2. A Baptist minister made friends with an Army captain stationed near the Chinese border. The captain was a Syrian Catholic from Kerala. The minister decided he ought to be a Catholic too, and the Baptists threw him out. So he looked up Prem Bhai and got him to come, and together they received the profession of faith of fifty-six former members of his congregation, with the result that now four or five villages around there are Catholic. The former minister met the captain at the Baptist chapel, because, since that was the only building in the neighborhood with a cross on it, the captain would go there on Sundays to say his prayers.

Saturday, June 12

Another book from Bede's library: *Trialogues at the Edge of the West: Chaos, Creativity, and the Resacralization of the World*, by Ralph Abraham, Terrence McKenna, and Rupert Sheldrake. For many years, the authors have frequented or resided at Esalen Institute, up the road from the Camaldolese hermitage in Big Sur. Sheldrake also spent more than a year at Shantivanam, writing his first book. He has donated these and many other books to Bede's library.

Monday, June 14

Life is dangerous and involves risk. Some people, for safety's sake, refuse to live life to the full. Striving to avoid the passion of concupiscence, they fall into the passion of fear.

Of course, one risks striving toward the opposite extreme. "All is permitted," said Saint Paul. "But," he adds, "not all is expedient." The real goal is wisdom acquired through the practice of discernment and discretion. However one strives, one must set out from the major premise that our nature and its appetites — irascible, concupiscible, noetic — are all good. They are Nature's message to us, and the message says, "God is good."

Tuesday, June 15

I awoke at 2:38 a.m. The candle kept going out, and I kept getting up to light it again.

What did my dream tell me?

They are interviewing an opera diva. She has successfully sung a difficult role. "But," she says, "not so well as I did thirteen years ago." Then she speaks of a famous tenor, whose most recent performance was in a religious role, not as Jesus but as a martyred priest, and she says, "He understands Jesus and the Gospel less well than he did then."

How well do I understand Jesus and the Gospel? I wonder whether it is a question of 'understanding' in view of 'successful performance'. The Bible says that Mary did not understand her Son.

People do not want to stand on slippery ground; our noetic appetite cannot tolerate unknowing. But perhaps God calls us to proceed on uncertain terrain and to trust in a mysterious guidance.

Think back, Thomas, to where you were, thirteen years ago.

Have I wasted my life by not living it? Or have I lost it by trying to keep it? In my mid-fifties, I ask myself whether I have lived, loved, and created. Only a part of me accepts my age; another part 'feels' young and thinks I still have time to make new choices and to create some good.

Have I loved God? Yes, but inconsistently. Or rather, I do think I have loved God with my whole being, but I have been unable to relate all my psychic structures to God and to the good that God wants from me for the sake of others. Above all, I have failed to manifest the image of benevolence and compassion toward all, which is the image of Jesus, the 'martyred priest' whom I inwardly hold up before my conscience.

Saturday, June 19
A white dog has been showing up in front of my hut. Apparently, the guest who stayed here while I was away used to feed him. Seeing that he was not aggressive, I began to talk to him. I told him, gesturing with my arms, that he may lie in the shade alongside the hut or on the concrete porch, but that he may never come inside. I also told him I will speak to him but will not touch him.

He is following these rules to the letter. In fact, he seems to have assumed the duty of guarding the hut. When other dogs appear, he bristles and growls, or else he gets off the porch and leads the dog away. When humans come, he goes away. On one occasion, he growled at a person who was coming to see me, and I think I know why...

Tuesday, June 22

Mass today at eleven, with the Vicar General of the Trichy diocese and the ex-pastors of Kulittalai parish, concluded the forty-day mourning period for Dom Bede.

I have finished reading (all from Bede's collection): Joseph Campbell's *Creative Mythology* (volume four of The Masks of God); *An Open Life*, interviews that Campbell gave on a radio program with Michael Toms; Ken Wilber's *No Boundary: Eastern and Western Approaches to Personal Growth* (an easy introduction to his 'spectrum psychology').

Martin has decided he cannot go to Chicago. I have asked him to write out the talk he was going to give at the Dom Bede commemoration there, and I shall read it.

A letter came today from Wayne Teasdale, a great friend of Bede. He is on the organizing committee for the Parliament of Religions at Chicago.

Monday, June 28

Another 'perennial theology' or 'universal wisdom' axiom: "The worst is over; the best is yet to come." In other words, eschatological optimism (cf. Beatrice Bruteau), which is the chief categorical expression of infused, anagogic hope. This is why we sing Saint Augustine's oxymoron at Easter: "O felix culpa, O vere necessarium Adae peccatum." (O happy fault, O truly necessary sin of Adam.)

Optimism is fine, as long as we keep in mind that the first human sin, whatever its 'matter', was certainly the worst, and that it is only of this first and worst sin that we can say 'Happy fault! Necessary sin!' Every subsequent sin, whatever its matter and gravity, is always unnecessary and unhappy.

Or is it? After all, Augustine did add to Saint Paul's saying, "All things work together for the good," the phrase, "etiam peccata — even sins".

Monday, July 12

Sunday, the feast of Saint Benedict, I wasted precious meditation time fantasizing about a monastery built in modular units, not individual huts but small, multi-room buildings constructed around a courtyard. Every so often these construction fantasies grip me, and I feel ambivalent about them. However, they may actually be of the nature of mandalas.

Today is Brother David Steindl-Rast's birthday. When I am in this ashram, I think of him, strange to say, as if he were living right near by. There is something in his monastic wisdom that Shantivanam needs, but which I seem unable to communicate.

I dreamt of another Benedictine, Pierre de Béthune, weary because of all his tasks and responsibilities and travels at the service of interreligious dialogue. Then of my mother, who is looking at me intently and giving me sage advice.

Today I think I have exhausted the current vein of fantasies about monastic structures. If anything good came from them, it was in grasping an image not so much of a building as of a quality of space, which the building serves to shape and sustain: groundedness and stability.

Sunday, July 18

Yesterday Christudas and Martin were out all day. I knew nothing about it. I came to Mass and sat waiting and waiting, until Father Augustine leaned over and whispered, "They're not here."

This morning I asked Christudas, as soon as I saw him, "Is Martin all right?" He realized no one had told me of their absence, and explained that he had gone to say Mass at a mission station, and Martin was in Bangalore for the Jubilee celebration of an elderly nun to whom he is close.

Of course if I were less withdrawn, I might get informed about things before they happen. However, try as I may, I do not succeed in feeling guilty about my withdrawn existence here and about passing my days in a hut 'doing nothing'.

I have, however, done much reading — I am forcing myself to finish Ken Wilber's *Up from Eden*, and I am continually irritated by his near-truths. Some of his points are well made, but others are vitiated by one or another fallacy and by his rigidly 'hierarchical and developmental' view of the human psyche and human society. His model of the 'seven-storey building' looks suspiciously old-paradigm.

There is also in Wilber, as in other 'New Age' literature, a subtle or not-so-subtle vein of anti-Semitism. For example: "And one may — it is a terrible realization — look in vain through Judeo-Christian-Islamic religion for any authentic trace of the touch of the subtle Goddess herself. And that, we will see, would become a perfect and terrifying comment on an entire civilization" (page 190). Later he claims that, in contrast with Christendom, there has never been a religious war in Buddhist history. By the way, where is the 'subtle Goddess' in Theravada Buddhism?

Thursday, July 22
This morning's rather discursive meditation centered on the Apocalypse, the last book in the Bible, and the realization that, from start to finish, you see the Feminine in it. Even the 'Son of Man' is depicted in female dress. Might not a woman have written this last book of the Bible? The decisive figures are the Whore, the Cosmic Mother, and the Bride; the faulty grammar and syntax of the Greek are those of one whose educational opportunities were limited — like a Galilean fisherman, but also like a woman. Who might the authoress be? One of the Marys — the Mother of Jesus, or Mary Magdalen, or Martha's sister?

Someone once said that Priscilla, a friend of St. Paul, may have written or edited the Letter to the Hebrews.

Sunday, July 25

With a massive effort of will-power, I have finished reading Wilber's *Up from Eden*. His theories — along with similar ones relating to the history of consciousness — are the most serious challenges to Christianity and personalist mysticism at the end of the Twentieth Century.

His weak points are evident; he bolsters his theses with pseudo-scholarship, forced citations of other authors, and over-dependence on secondary sources, even of quite minor value, like newspaper book reviews and popular anthologies. He insists so much on a 'hierarchical and developmental' (I add: 'elitist') view of human history, that he constantly risks falling into the fallacies of Positivism, as if to say, "We are better because we come later."

Wilber can be challenged and countered by exposing his questionable readings of Vedanta, Mahayana Buddhism, and especially Gnosticism, which he identifies as 'esoteric Christianity'— the only valid kind as far as he is concerned. In general, you can point to the shaky and fragmentary data on which he and other 'historians of consciousness' base their theories. He is vulnerable to the criticism of 'involutionary theories' and 'loveless mysticism' that Pierre Teilhard de Chardin leveled at certain Asian spiritualities (but did he understand them? — see Ursula King, *Towards a New Mysticism: Teilhard de Chardin and Eastern Religions*). Finally, to Wilber's thought you can also apply the usual critique of Hegelian and similar 'Great Chain of Being' systems. This critique is not addressed to him solely from the standpoint of Christian orthodoxy but above all from that of progressive social thought and Liberation Theology.

In *Up from Eden*, on page 310, for the first and only time in the book, Wilber makes a slight nod toward love and compassion as a constant in the evolutionary process.

Sunday, August 1

I am departing for the United States: first, California, then

Chicago and the Parliament of Religions, and finally the monastery outside New Boston, New Hampshire, which the Camaldolese recently acquired and where the Bede Griffiths Trust will meet.

At Trichy airport, a customs officer, who lives near Shantivanam, allowed me to sit in the arrivals area (no seating in the departure zone). I have almost four hours to wait before my flight to Colombo.

From a word here and there, I can tell that the customs staff are asking their colleague about this ashram: Is it Catholic? Does the bishop approve? Tamilians, whether Hindus or Christians, tend to be quite conservative.

Yesterday, I finished reading a book on Monchanin, which tells of his last few years at the parish in Kulittalai and with Le Saux at Shantivanam, and of his death in a Paris suburb.

Monday, August 2
At the Sri Lanka airport hotel, some distance from the city of Colombo.

I never knew there were all-Christian zones on this island. Eight percent of the total population are Christians, most of them Catholics. All along the way from the airport to the hotel, you imagine that you are in the Philippines. No Buddhas, no Shivas, no Kalis, only crucifixes, pseudo-Gothic churches, roadside Mary shrines. Even the hotel bus has a rosary hanging from the rear-view mirror.

On the way, we passed a festive procession celebrating a small, overdressed Madonna perched atop an automobile, also overdressed. In fact, you could hardly tell it was an automobile, rather than a scaled-down model of Juggernaut's Chariot. On arrival, the bellhop turned on the one and only radio station in my room (there was no television), and behold, a dramatization of John chapter four, Jesus with the Samaritan woman.

Realizations this morning: That Jesus has irremediably

wounded me, but I belong to him whatever. That love is messy, just as dying is messy; when you die you drop as and where you are, and it's not nice or neat in any way, just as love is not neat and not always nice, because you fall in love where and as you are, when you meet the person you are to love. That authentic religion without miracles is non-existent, no matter what idea — old-paradigm or new — you may have about miracles, what they are, and how and under what conditions they happen.

The white dog at the ashram apparently understood, yesterday morning, that I was leaving and saying good-bye to him.

Epilogue

On Retreat at Shantivanam, 1993 – 2004

I returned to the ashram in November 1993, and I spent several months there every year, to 2004. I continued to keep a diary. Sister Marie-Louise invited me to live in a more secluded hut on her side of the path, but I joined in the ashram prayers and lunch every day.

1993 and 1994 were a time of grieving — the grief of the Indian members of the ashram community, for whom Dom Bede had been a father and guru, and the grief of British, European, and Australian guests, on whose inner shadows and longing for spirituality Bede had shed his peaceful light. I counseled my Indian brothers and received much wise counsel from Marie-Louise. But I was unable to help the guests.

A few of them, learning that I was from a monastery in Italy, supposed that I had been sent by Rome to 'turn the ashram into an orthodox Catholic monastery'. I knew that this thought pained and angered them, and at times, waves of their negativity swept over me and filled me with deep anguish. Anonymous letters were written about me and to me.

I had no such 'institutional' project. I was just there, giving brief talks and occasional homilies, but most days I remained cloistered in the hut among Marie-Louise's coconut palms. Probably some of their projections could have been dissipated had I come more regularly to the ashram tea circle. My penchant for solitude reflected even more unfavorably on me than did the anonymous complaints.

One day in 1994, I met with Christudas, Martin, and Marie-Louise, and asked them if I should leave and not come back to the ashram any more. They insisted that I stay and comforted me with their encouragement and affection. So at least I found peace in myself, even though I seemed unable to give peace to others. The experience both reassured me — I knew I belonged to the ashram — and chastened me. I realized I had little of Dom Bede's grace and charisma, although I share his faith in the cosmic Christ and his love for India.

Whether or not my presence there made any difference, the 'Indian Benedictine Ashram' at Shantivanam has, in fact, continued to live and grow, and so have I. My retreats at the ashram were longer than in the past: twice a year, two or three months at a time, in the three years following Bede's passing, and then every year until 2004. I continued to learn about India and myself, and I gave teachings to the novices and sometimes even to the guests. Why did I not just move there? I would have done so, had I not been committed to teaching my yearly course on Hindu and Buddhist Monasticism at Sant'Anselmo in Rome. I was also involved in the general council of the Camaldolese Benedictines, an office that fell to me without my seeking it.

We — the ashram's Indian members and our monastics in Italy and California — believe that Shantivanam has kept faith with the original purpose of Monchanin, Le Saux, and Griffiths. 1995 brought many guests to Shantivanam for the one-hundredth birth anniversary of Jules Monchanin. We celebrated the event with scholarly conferences in France and India, but the contributions to the Indian gathering included numerous testimonies from those who had known Monchanin personally and from those who, like myself, had met him through his writings. We edited and published the scholarly papers and personal testimonies in two volumes.

In 2006, we commemorated Dom Bede's birth centenary at New Camaldoli in Big Sur and at the ashram. I gave a paper in Big Sur, but did not join those gathering at Shantivanam. We look forward to commemorating Henri Le Saux, Abhishiktananda, on the centenary of his birth in 2010.

The ashram community is growing now. Three novices from the local Catholic community have made their final vows, and one of them has been ordained. Most of the guests are Indians — lay people, religious sisters, and clergy. Numerous seekers still come from Europe, the United States, and elsewhere to discover or rediscover the beauty of the place, the aura of serene love and harmony that the three 'wise men from the West', Monchanin, Le Saux, and Griffiths, radiate from their tombs next to the little temple. The 'forest of peace' they planted and watered still flourishes today, thanks to the faithfulness of its monastic members and its many friends, in India and abroad. I thank God for the great gifts the ashram has given me, and for the hope that perhaps I have given something to its life today and its future possibilities.

NOTES

1. 'Bede' is the new name he received in the monastery; he was born Alan Griffiths. 'Dom' is a monastic title given to monks who are either ordained or preparing for ordination.

2. I actually read the book in French: *Initiation à la spiritualité des Upanishads: 'Vers l'Autre Rive'* (Saint-Vincent-sur-Jabron, France: Editions Présence, 1979). The quotations are my own translation; Abhishiktananda published an English version in India, but I have preferred, for various reasons, the final revision of the text in the author's native tongue.

3. Cf. Henri Le Saux O.S.B. Swami Abhishiktananda, *op. cit.*, p. 196.

4. Cf. *op. cit.*, p. 169.

5. *Ibid.*

6. Ghurye, G. S.. *Indian Sadhus* (Bombay: Popular Prakashan, 1964), p. 16.

7. Cf. Abhishiktananda, *op. cit.*, pp. 180-181.

8. *Op. cit.*, p. 176.

9. *Ibid.*

10. Cf. *op. cit.*, p. 183.

11. Cf. *op. cit.*, pp. 183-193.

12. John 4:21.

13. Cf. Psalm 18:11.

14. "Heaven is other people": turning around a phrase in Jean-Paul Sartre's play *Huis clos* (No Exit): "*L'enfer, c'est les autres* — Hell is other people."

15. Turning around Augustine's prayer: "*Fecisti nos ad te* — You made us for yourself."

16. Colossians 2:9.

17. John 1:12 and 14.

18. Paramahansa Yogananda, *Autobiography of a Yogi* (Los Angeles: Self-Realization Fellowship, 1972), p. 237.

19. In the two years that followed his recovery, Bede made a series of trips to Europe, Australia, and the United States that brought his message of dialogue and spiritual renewal to millions of persons, through public lectures, television interviews, and documentaries.

B O O K S

O is a symbol of the world, of oneness and unity. In different
cultures it also means the "eye", symbolizing knowledge and
insight. We aim to publish books that are accessible, constructive
and that challenge accepted opinion, both that of academia and
the "moral majority".

Our books are available in all good English language
bookstores worldwide. If you don't see the book on the shelves
ask the bookstore to order it for you, quoting the ISBN number
and title. Alternatively you can order online (all major online
retail sites carry our titles) or contact the distributor in the
relevant country, listed on the copyright page.

See our website www.o-books.net for a full list of over 400
titles, growing by 100 a year.

And tune in to myspiritradio.com for our book review radio show,
hosted by June-Elleni Laine, where you can listen to the authors
discussing their books.

MySpiritRadio